The Rosellas

Jim Hayward

Published 1995 by the Aviculturist Publications
Carterton Breeding Aviaries
Brize Norton Road
Carterton OXFORD OX18 3HW
ENGLAND

ISBN 0-9519098-1-9

DEDICATION

To the parrakeet breeders of Australia, Europe and Britain in appreciation of the help received by the author in the preparation of this book.

Acknowledgement and Thanks

ACKNOWLEDGEMENT AND THANKS for information regarding the subjects covered in this book (received through personal conversations, letters and photographs over past years), are due to the following, with prior apologies for omissions:

Australia: Keith Gallagher, Peter Chapman, John Raymond, Stan Sindel, John Vaughn, Tom Donald, John Wells, Gordon Dosser, Todd Osborne, Gary Lees, Ron Hastings, Bill Boyd and Hugo Austla.

England: Alan Oliver (Cotswolds), Fred Brooks (South East), J. Woods (South East), Gordon Woodward (Cotswolds), John Kenrick (Midlands), F. White (North Midlands) and R.White (North Midlands).

Europe: Ernst Kalf (Holland), Herman Zomer (Holland), Han van Dooran (Holland), E. Adams (Belgium) and Povl Jorgensen (Denmark).

South Africa: Dr David Russell, and Derek Dosser.

THE BLUE GUM ROAD: a vehicle disappears in a cloud of dust up the deliberately rocky road; the lack of a tarmac surface dissuades all but the most essential traffic from traversing this conservation area west of Sydney, thus reducing disturbance to wildlife, which includes parrakeets, lorikeets and cockatoos.

Contents

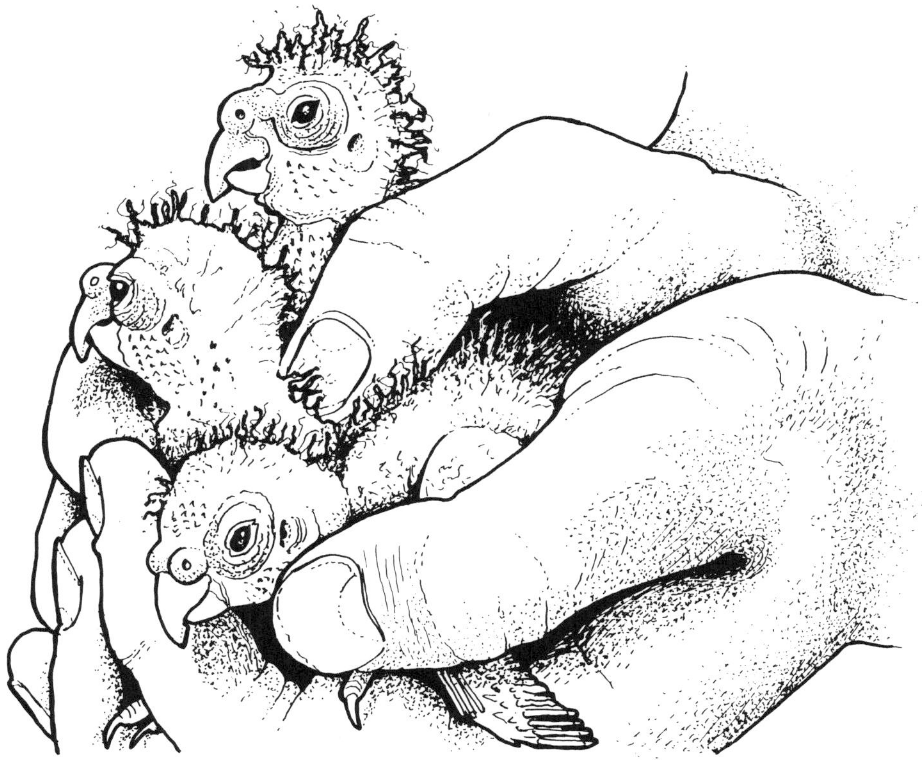

TO ENCOURAGE the Breeding of Birds

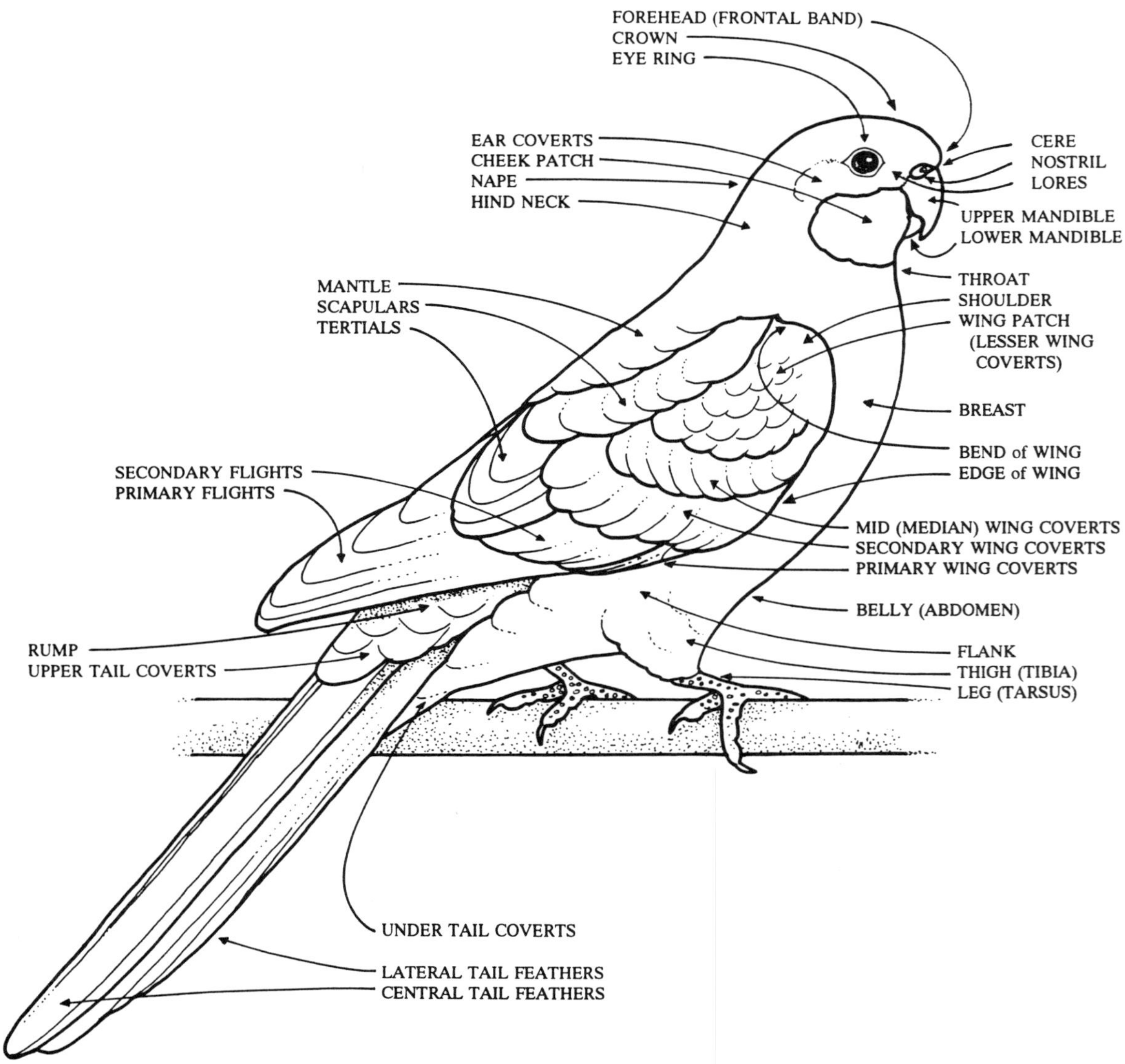

The Main External Features of the Rosella

Introduction

THE VIVID KALEIDOSCOPE of colours displayed in the plumage of the most common species of Rosella has been the temptation and stimulus for many a prospective aviculturist to step into the absorbing world of the parrakeet breeder. Eight species make up the genus *Platycercus* and they are found naturally on the island continent of Australia, its island of Tasmania and some smaller coastal islands.

Their popular name is derived from 'Rose-hill' parrakeet, from the area of Sydney in which some of the first examples of the genus were originally observed by British settlers in Australia; over many years it was shortened from 'Rosehill' Parrakeet to 'Rosehiller' and finally 'Rosella'. Initially only describing one species - the Eastern Rosella - it gradually came to represent all the members of the genus *Platycercus*.

The Rosellas and their close relatives have - for the most - become well established in British, European, American and South African aviaries since they were banned from export of their native shores several decades ago, and are popular aviary birds in their homeland of Australia. As well as information and illustrations regarding: the Rosellas, the species and sub-species of the genus *Barnardius*, the single species of the genus *Purpureicephalus*, and the existing colour varieties of these birds, examples of possible future developments in colour varieties have also been included in this book.

Some breeders are against colour mutations, I am all for them and am pleased when I see them being established within aviary bred strains; not just because colour varieties enrich aviculture and increase popularity in a species, but also because they mean that the strains are becoming more and more domesticated; this confirms and consolidates their belonging and retention within the sphere of the bird breeder. Whether retaining sub-species or increasing the number of colour forms within a species, as far as I am concerned, variety in the birds we keep truly is the spice of life.

However, hybridization is ever present, and the birds produced are frequently fertile and stronger than the original parent species, which means they pose a threat to the purity of those species and can be a damaging factor to our aviary strains. Distinctive sub-species can easily be lost through hybridization and this has happened with Rosellas in Britain; cross breeding to instil a colour variety from one species into another has been commonly attempted in the past with other genera of psittacine birds, but this practice must be warned against and resisted. Beginners especially must beware purchasing such hybrids and be advised of the harmful consequences of widespread hybridization.

The work on this book really started in nineteen eighty-seven when I began painting colour plates of the Rosellas and their varieties; an eye problem held me up and before the gouache and water colour paintings were all completed the work had to be left. Afterwards, it was found necessary to make a completely new set of illustrations, but, before this, it was realised that it would be sensible to first publish a separate book covering the whole topic of colour varieties in psittacine birds, as the subject would be too complex to include in a work on a small group of parrakeets; therefore, all the genetics and breeding programmes needed to produce the primary, combination and compound varieties of the Rosellas and associated parrakeets are thoroughly covered in the publication which resulted - ***The Manual of Colour Breeding*** - and it should be used in conjunction with this book - ***The Rosellas*** - if colour varieties are the breeder's main interest.

To many bird breeders of our day, the Rosella group of parrakeets most especially represents the very essence of Australia, and of course these and their closely allied genera are unique to the island continent; yet they have been bred here in Britain for so many of their generations that most species are firmly established as a cherished part of our own avicultural heritage - may this always be so.

THE 'UNDER-WING STRIPE' does *not* provide a conclusive method of sexing Rosellas; the intimations of its presence or absence in the various species is explained in the text.

The 'Under-wing Stripe'

1. *The Species & Sub-species of Genus Platycercus*

The EASTERN or RED ROSELLA
Platycercus eximius

Australia: Eastern Rosella, Common Rosella, Red-headed Rosella, Rosehill Parrakeet, or Bundalcck (Aboriginal).
France: Perruche omnicolore.
Germany: Rosellasittich.
Holland: Rosella.

Length: $12^1/_4$in, 31cm.
Weight: cock 97-120gm, hen 90gm.

THE MOST well known of the genus *Platycercus* is the **Eastern Rosella**; beside the nominate sub-species there are two other sub-species, the **Tasmanian Eastern Rosella** *(Platycercus eximius diemenensis)*, and the brilliant **Golden-mantled Rosella** *(Platycercus eximius cecilae)*. In British aviculture, any Tasmanian Eastern Rosellas have long ago been engulfed by the commoner and most numerous Easterns, while the true Golden-mantled must now be considered an unappreciated rarity.

Description
In the Eastern Rosella, the head, upper breast, vent and under-tail coverts are bright red; the lower breast is yellow, and the belly green - with feathers of breast and belly having faint dark edges. The feathers of the mantle, scapulars and tertials are blackish edged with yellow-green, the rump is light green and central tail feathers are green shading to dark blue at their edges; the lateral tail feathers are dark blue at their bases, shading to pale blue and finally becoming whitish at their tips. There is a characteristic black band on the upper wing followed by rich ultramarine blue on the outer wing, the primaries are blackish lined with blue on their outer edges. The distinctive cheek patches are white with just a suggestion of blue at their borders, the irides are dark brown, bill pale grey and feet brown-grey.

The Golden-mantled Rosella is even more brilliant than the nominate race, with vivid scarlet replacing the red; the mantle feathers are edged with orange yellow, and the rump is turquoise blue.

The Tasmanian Eastern has a rounder and bulkier appearance, possibly because it carries more underdown as protection against the colder Tasmanian climate. Its colours are more brilliant than the common mainland form, it has a more noticeable yellow patch at the nape of the neck wedged between the red of the head and the beginnings of the mantle feathers, and the white cheek patches are larger, spreading down onto the throat and across the sides of the face.

Parrakeet breeder Keith Gallagher from New South Wales sent me recent photographs of a mixed flock of Rosellas and Galahs feeding on the grass at the back of his friend's home in Tasmania; with Galahs alongside for comparison, the large size and robust figure of this sub-species of the Eastern is clear to see.

Sexing
Easterns are easily sexed by the brighter and more sharply defined colours of the cock as opposed to the rather toned down coloration of the hen; the red on his head reaches further down the back of the neck than does that of the hen, and is sharply delineated at the point where it meets the black and yellow feathering. The bill and head of the cock is larger than

that of the hen, as are the cheek patches; these differences can also be clearly seen even in fledglings, but youngsters are similar in depth of colour to the hen.

A pale spot on the undersurface of the flight feathers makes up an under-wing stripe which is usually present in adult hens but lacking in adult cocks; it is also present in both sexes of immature birds which - like adult hens - are duller in comparison with their fathers.

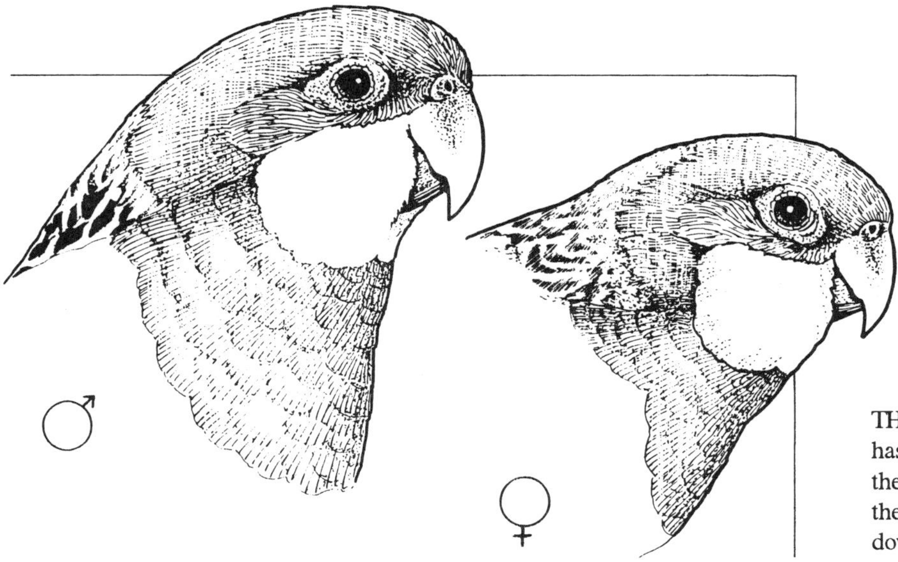

THE COCK EASTERN ROSELLA has a larger head and bill than the hen, is brighter in colour, and the red of his head reaches further down into the nape of his neck.

Age of Maturity

Both cocks and hens of only one year old - youngsters from a pair's first brood of the season - will attempt to breed, usually a week or more later than older adults. If the first clutch is infertile, a fully adult hen is capable of laying again in about two weeks.

Distribution and Habits in the Wild

There is a broad band of distribution of the Eastern Rosella on mainland Australia, from south-eastern South Australia, through Victoria into New South Wales; the Golden-mantled type becomes evident from the area of the Hunter River Valley in New South Wales and carries on northwards into south-eastern Queensland. The Tasmanian sub-species is confined to eastern areas of the island. Easterns have been introduced into New Zealand and populations exist on both North and South Islands.

This Rosella is usually seen in family groups or pairs; it lives in areas of open woodland, and trees adjacent to waterways; it is seen in orchards, parks and gardens and has actually gained advantage from the clearing of large areas of thicker forest for agricultural purposes - especially the areas set aside for growing of cereals. Introduced seeding weeds, such as the irreplaceable and ever useful dandelion *(Taraxacum vulgaria)*, are also welcome additions to the plentiful native fare - as far as these birds are concerned. Whether feeding amongst foliage or on the ground, their harlequin plumage serves as good camouflage despite its brilliance.

Breeding Condition

In Europe, the first signs of breeding condition are seen in March, and hens usually come into lay during April. With nervous hens, nest inspections should not be carried out during incubation and while nestlings are very small. There can often be a race to reach the nest between the returning Rosella hen and the curious owner and this can be disruptive to the breeding efforts of all the aviary occupants. Hens can be greatly dependent on their cocks, and hatchlings may be allowed to die unless the cock does his proper share of the nesting chores by regularly feeding his hen.

Nesting in the Wild

When deciding on a nest site, Eastern Rosellas will choose hollowed out limbs or trunks of trees, but are quite willing to make do with telegraph poles or rotting stumps of fence posts; once possession is claimed the cock guards the site against other nest seekers, allowing the hen to complete her work in excavating and altering the entrance and hollow to her satisfaction. His aggressive actions towards interlopers include the tail wagging of the courtship ritual, rapid chattering and a thrusting forward of his shoulders with bill tucked into his throat feathers, if this is not enough to scare off the interloper, he hurls himself at the enemy with great fury. In the southern hemisphere, the Easterns commence nesting during October and carry on into December.

Though clutches of nine eggs and even more are known, five eggs is normal, incubation takes eighteen or nineteen days, and during this time the hen leaves the nest seldom more than a couple of times a day to defecate and drink. The cock feeds the hen and - for around ten days - she in turn feeds this twice regurgitated food to the nestlings; after this time an increasing amount of food is needed to sustain the young and then the cock will also help to feed them directly. The fledglings - which have yellowish bills and may still have fronds of down sticking out from between the feathers on their heads and backs - leave the nest when about five weeks old; they often remain in company with their parents as a family group until the next breeding season. Nestling feather is shed in the autumn for a brighter intermediate plumage, but the final polish of full brilliant colour is not attained until the following year.

Colour Varieties

Despite the fact that this parrakeet has been such a common avicultural subject for so many years, colour varieties are a relatively new aspect for breeders of the Eastern Rosella and, though - in general - their great potential seems to have been missed by present day breeders, they are sure to become an increasing source of interest to parrakeet enthusiasts of this decade and the next.

The commonest colour variety in the Eastern Rosella is the **Dilute** which is *Autosomal Recessive* in its inheritance. Its effect gives partial to almost complete lack of melanin and - at its best - changes green plumage to yellow with a lime tinge; the black of mantle feathers is reduced to greygreen or pale green; all red plumage is retained and lightened. The overall effect of this factor is variable, with some birds almost completely lacking melanin on mantle and wings - resulting in practically yellow backs. The variability in individuals may be a result of selective breeding or even of two or more similar but separate mutations which are *allelomorphic*. On the continent the Dilute is described as '**Pastel**' or '**Yellow**'.

The **Lutino** Eastern (Ino factor) has been recorded for many years but - at present - is still a great rarity; there are reports of both *Sex-linked Recessive* and *Autosomal Recessive* forms and this is sure to cause some confusion if they are unknowingly mixed together. Its effect gives total lack of melanin, producing yellow, cream and white plumage in place of green, black and blue; red plumage is made lighter; the eyes are red; bill and feet are flesh coloured.

Cinnamon - as is usual with the variety - is *Sex-linked Recessive* in its inheritance; its effect causes melanin black to change to melanin brown, and this makes black areas - especially on the mantle - range in colour from brown to fawn. The continental type of Cinnamon Eastern is known as '**Isabel**', in Australia a darker type of Cinnamon exists.

The *Autosomal Dominant* **Pied** is well established on the continent, its effect causes melanin to be lacking in patches, revealing yellow and white ground colour, but elimination of red in variegated areas can be looked on as a detrimental trait; individuals which show almost complete variegation lack practically all red colour with ground colour reduced to just yellow, cream and white. On the continent, specimens with large areas of variegation on the wings are described as '**Silver-winged**' or '**White-winged**'.

On the occasions that the **Ruby** Eastern Rosella is advertised for sale here in Britain specimens are often overlooked because they are generally described simply as '**Red Rosellas**' which - though giving an adequate picture of their appearance - leads many people to dismiss the birds as being normal Easterns; this name was used to describe the nominate race in the past. The Ruby is *Sex-linked Recessive* in its inheritance and its effect is to cause spread of red colour over all of the underparts and rump as well as most of the edging of the mantle feathers; in one form of this variety the central tail feathers become dusky pink with a dark quill, while the blue and white colours of the lateral tail feathers are retained, along with the blues and blacks of the wings and the white of the cheek patches; examples have also been seen with central tail feathers darkening from yellow at their bases, shading through green and ending in blue at their tips.

This variety has also been described as '**Opaline**', however, Opaline in the budgerigar describes characteristics which create a 'V' pattern at the mantle and gives spread of melanin based coloration to the normally ground colour based edging on mantle feathers; in the Ruby Eastern no 'V' is created and the extreme change in appearance is not due to spread of melanin pigment but mostly to replacement of yellow ground by red ground.

Known of and illustrated from wild specimens in Gould's time - when it was thought to be a distinct species and named the **Fiery Parrakeet** *(Platycercus ignitus)* - this variety could be the oldest wild occurring colour mutation parrakeet. Well known Australian parrot breeders - brothers Syd and Jack Smith - established this variety at their aviaries in Victoria after many years of work.

Care must be taken to check the validity of examples of the Ruby variety; I have seen Eastern x Pennant hybrids which simulate this effect very closely, even down to white cheek patches. If fertile cock or hen hybrids were paired to Normal Easterns, a degree of the Pennant coloration would be present in the young - with a true Ruby Eastern the Sex-linked pattern of inheritance would come into play and give proof if the bird were genuine.

One of the most unusual and recently established mutations of the Eastern Rosella is the **Melanistic** which is of course predominantly black, presumably due to an increase in melanin production; the variety has been established in New South Wales by Raymond and Joelle Marshall. This is the only truly melanistic mutant variety so far reported in psittacine birds, though it has a direct parallel with the naturally occurring melanistic phase of Stella's Lorikeet *(Charmosyna papou stellae)*. The Black Stella's Lorikeet has established itself in the wild alongside its original predominantly red wild form.

The Melanistic Eastern is an *Autosomal Recessive* and its effect causes a spread of black or blackish plumage over most of the bird. White cheek patches are still present but they contain flecks of black; the underside of the tail is blackish; some red is retained on the head and breast, but hens are blacker in appearance than cocks.

The latest mutation to be reported in the Eastern is a true **Blue**, with red and yellow ground colours completely missing and replaced by white, but with blacks and blues retained.

Once these primary varieties are all well established and wide spread, there is sure to be competition to produce new colours by combination. For example, **Cinnamon Ruby, Dilute Ruby, Cinnamon Melanistic** (which should be shades of brown and fawn with red on the breast and head), and a combination of Ruby and Ino - **Rubino**. If a **Marine** variety also occurs, as with other Australian Parrakeets, then a **Creamino** could be produced with salmon pink replacing red, and cream replacing yellow; carrying on from this a compound variety could be made up of Marine, Ruby and Ino which would create a Rosella coloured predominantly salmon pink with white and cream wings. Futuristic maybe, though not only possible but clearly probable.

The MEALY or BLUE ROSELLA
Platycercus adscitus

Australia: Mealy Rosella, Blue Rosella, White-headed Rosella or Moreton Bay Rosella.
France: Perruche à bleu *(Platycercus adscitus adscitus)*, Perruche à tête pale *(Platycercus adscitus palliceps)*
Germany: Blauwangenrosella *(Platycercus adscitus adscitus)*, Blaszkopfrosella *(Platycercus adscitus palliceps)*
Holland: Blauwwang Rosella *(Platycercus adscitus adscitus)*, Bleekkop Rosella *(Platycercus adscitus palliceps)*.

Length: $11^3/_4$in, 30cm *(Platycercus adscitus adscitus)*, $12^1/_2$in, 32cm, *(Platycercus adscitus palliceps)*.
Weight: cock 100-105gm, hen 98gm *(Platycercus adscitus adscitus)*, cock 131gm, hen 112gm *(Platycercus adscitus palliceps)*.

THE PARRAKEET we call the '**Mealy Rosella**' is - in its brightest and most colourful form - probably the result of hybridization between the nominate race and its sub-species, or at least originates from a transitional type. In their extreme forms, these two differ greatly.

Description
The **Blue-cheeked Rosella** *(Platycercus adscitus adscitus)* - now an avicultural rarity outside of Australia - has yellow on its upper breast and violet-blue underparts, with the edging of its black mantle feathers shading from pale yellow at the nape of the neck to greenish blue across its back - the rump varies from yellowish bronze to pale bluish green. The **Pale-headed Rosella** *(Platycercus adscitus palliceps)* - in its purest form - has an insipid body colour shading from pale yellowish blue green on the breast to pale blue on the underparts; it has a pale blue rump and a rich golden yellow edging to its mantle feathers. It is understandable that birds which incorporate the most colourful features of both types have always found more favour, but this has been to the detriment of the exceedingly small British stock of Blue-cheekeds. As far as I recall, the only British breeder to establish a pure strain of these birds was the late Ron Godwin of Cheltenham, in the late nineteen-sixties; on his death the small stock was scattered hither and thither, to be completely absorbed into the general Mealy population throughout Britain - and probably Europe.

As with the Eastern, both forms have scarlet under-tail coverts; the central tail feathers are green shading to dark blue at their edges; lateral tail feathers are dark blue at their bases, shading to pale blue and finally whitish at their tips; the under-tail is sky blue. The characteristic black band on the upper wing is present, followed by rich ultramarine blue on the outer wing, the primaries are blackish lined with blue on their outer edges. The irides are dark brown, bill pale grey and feet brown-grey. In the Pale-headed, the cheek patches are white with just a suggestion of blue at their edges, but - as its name indicates - the lower portion of those of the Blue-cheeked are ultramarine, the colour spreading down the sides of the neck.

Breeders are often surprised to find that their nestling Mealies have varying amounts of rusty red on their heads, and are worried in case this indicates adulteration with Eastern blood. When the youngsters moult into adult plumage the rusty colour disappears, but, with some adults, just a fleck or two remain on the forehead or crown. Young Blue-cheekeds are less prone to this discolouration. Hybridization between Pale-headeds and Easterns occurs in the wild. It is generally easy to sex adult Mealies by their appearance; cocks have quite flat heads, large bills, a deeper colour and a bouncy boisterous manner. Hens have rounder heads, smaller bills, a slightly subdued colour and are wary and respectful of their partners at most times of the year.

Unpredictable Nature

Amongst a genus well known for pugnacious behaviour, not only towards rivals of the same sex but also regarding cocks towards their own hens, in my experience, the Mealy is the most violent; some cock Mealies develop an almost psychopathic nature when the breeding season comes around, chasing their hens to exhaustion, biting their feet and heads, and - worst of all - even ripping out their upper mandibles to the root; the species is adversely represented by a good peppering of wife beaters and wife murderers. Where the cock is of such a nature, there is some skill involved in bringing the cock and his hen into breeding condition at the same time, but when this is achieved, an aggressive cock must be watched carefully to see that he does not treat his young family in the same way has he would treat his wife. The Mealy cock also takes a wicked delight in acting as a scaremonger to the rest of the inhabitants of an aviary block by giving needless alarm calls and dashing about the flight sending all the other parrakeets close by into a mad panic.

Distribution and Habitat

The Blue-cheeked Rosella is less numerous than the Pale-headed, it is found in Cape York Peninsula in north-eastern Queensland, spreading south as far as a roughly diagonal line leading along the Mitchell River across to Cairns in the east; from this area specimens begin to take on the appearance of the Pale-headed Rosella. The sub-species carries on south again to north-eastern New South Wales, where its range extends into that of the Golden mantled Rosella; not surprisingly - in overlapping areas - evidence of hybridization between the two can be seen in adult specimens of the Pale-headed Rosella which have rusty red on the forehead, often spreading over the crown or the entire head.

In its homeland, the Mealy lives in open woodland, grasslands, and even in the parks and gardens of towns. As with the Eastern, its plumage patterns make it inconspicuous in the moving leafy shadows of the tree tops, where it finds ample sustenance amongst a bounty of budding, flowering, fruiting, seeding foliage, to say nothing of the nectar, and the insect species which are attracted as a consequence of this produce. Also, like its more brilliant cousin, it is frequently seen feeding amongst shrubs and at ground level on seeding plants and grasses - very little that is worth gnawing, chewing or cracking escapes its attention.

Colour Varieties

At present there are no known established strains of colour varieties in the Mealy Rosella; **Pied** examples exist in Australia which - like all Pied varieties in Australian and Asiatic Parrakeets - changes red ground colour to yellow, resulting in the loss of the scarlet under-tail and vent when the Pied effect has spread to this area. It is not known if the Australian Pied Mealy can reproduce itself, but Mealies with white spreading from the face down the breast - and sometimes with a white flight feather or two - could often be seen in England during the nineteen seventies; these drew no special attention from the breeders of the day.

It can well be imagined that a **Blue** variety of the Mealy would be a very popular variety once established; at present I know of no examples but it is possible to make a representation of such a bird and this I have done, as well as making a projection of a **Lutino** - as can be seen in the colour plates.

BROWN'S or The NORTHERN ROSELLA
Platycercus venustus

Australia: Brown's Rosella, Northern Rosella, Smutty Rosella, or Beautiful Parrakeet.
France: Perruche de Brown.
Germany: Brownsittich, or Schwarzcopfrosella.
Holland: Brown Rosella.

Length: 11in, 28cm.
Weight: cock 92-112gm, hen 88-92gm.

THE STRIKING **Brown's Rosella** *(Platycercus venustus venustus)* is a fine beauty from the tropical areas of northern Australia. Though still considered a rare and difficult subject to breed in Britain - mainly because of its well known inclination to nest in the European autumn - young pairs become available from time to time, at a price.

Numbers have increased within aviculture over the past decade or so, and there are now instances of spring breedings; in fact, at least one British breeder has had the luck to see a breeding pair go to nest in both autumn and spring! Hybridization between Brown's and Eastern, Pale-headed or Blue-cheeked Rosellas was carried out in past years during attempts to instil a spring breeding instinct. Evidence of this adulteration can be seen in red flecking on heads and other mis-markings in some individuals. Nevertheless, Australian breeders tell me that wild specimens can also show red flecking.

Description
Its wings and tail have all the typical colours and markings of the Eastern and the Mealy (though the central tail feathers show less green and tend more towards dark blue); the unique plumage feature which sets it apart from the rest of the genus is its sooty black head. Otherwise it is coloured as follows: white cheeks tinged blue, creamy yellow feathers on breast and belly edged with black (most heavily on the upper breast), black mantle feathers edged with cream, and vent and under-tail coverts scarlet.

There is a sub-species recognized from the western areas of its range known as the **Blue-cheeked Northern** or the **Kimberley Northern Rosella** *(Platycercus venustus hilli)*; from its name we see that it has more blue on the cheeks than the nominate sub-species, but individuals may also have blue shading across the breast and mantle feathers - they are also reckoned to be slightly smaller.

Distribution
The Brown's is found in northern Western Australia and tropical Northern Territory (spreading over the Queensland boundary), as well as some islands off the northern coast. It is generally regarded as being uncommon and usually seen only in pairs or small family groups instead of in flocks. Brown's prefer to live in woods close to water, and their present day scarcity is blamed on the clearing of woodland to provide grazing. In contrast, an increase in numbers of the Eastern is credited to the spread of agriculture, the accompanying irrigation - which provides water where there was none - and the resulting crops which provide this parrakeet with extra food.

As well as searching the ground for seeding grasses and plants, and probably taking insects, they make full use of the blossoms, nectar, buds, seeds and fruit of their homelands, frequenting stands of acacias, melaleucas and eucalypts which - in the north - are mainly orange and red flowering, whereas white and yellow flowering species predominate in the south.

In their wild secluded places, Brown's Rosellas keep themselves quiet and watchful and are quicker to avoid interlopers than the more tolerant Easterns, they also tend to produce smaller clutches than their close relatives.

Breeding in Britain

Reporting in the magazine of *the Parrot Society*, an anonymous British breeder of Brown's described his experiences with this Rosella. His birds hatched occasional young, but all died because the hen ceased brooding the hatchlings after only three to four days. Finally, serious thought was given to persuading the pair to breed and in the September of the year the birds were moved to an aviary consisting of an outer flight measuring twelve feet long (3.65m) by three feet wide (.91m) and an inside flight of the same dimensions. Though nest-boxes were provided in both flights, the hen Brown's chose to nest in the outside flight. These boxes contained false bottoms lined with asbestos and were wired up with holders for a pair of forty watt electric light bulbs.

Even though the hen was moulting she had begun to stay in the nest, and - at the end of October - the cock began enthusiastic courtship displays. When the hen was out of the nest - on the first of December - a quick inspection discovered a full clutch of five eggs, with three being fertile. By the ninth of December two had hatched, and the light bulbs in the bottom of the nest were then switched on. There is no mention of a thermo-stat to prevent overheating, but the heat was sure to dissipate very quickly in an outside flight during the severe cold of December and January.

Both cock and hen fed the hatchlings, mainly on orange and apple, ignoring the soaked seed and soaked brown bread sprinkled with glucose and *'Bemax'* which had been provided. Despite her previous disinterest in brooding, this time the hen spent a lot of time in the nest. The hard seed mixture contained the usual sunflower, various millets (including spray), hemp and canary seed. The nesting was successful and two young were reared to independence.

Essex breeder Fred Brooks has persevered with this difficult species for a long time but only began to breed them with success seven or more years ago. As has been explained previously, one of the difficulties with Brown's in our hemisphere is their insistence on beginning nesting in autumn - the exact opposite of the other Rosellas which are spring breeders. At the Brooks' aviaries some individuals in the strain have been found to nest not only in autumn, but - as an extra bonus - in spring as well. Some immatures have red flecking on their heads, some yellow; cocks lose this colour at the first moult but some hens retain head speckling. The best year so far for Brown's was in nineteen eighty-eight when two pairs produced twelve young. It was found that the hen Brown's brooded their hatchlings for five days only, and Mr Brooks found that even a heated nest-box was of no use in preventing the loss of young because of this trait. The birds are housed in outside flights the year round with no artificial heat provided in winter. The practice of hand-rearing finally provided a break through, and a number of young Brown's were reared over the following years. Despite the current disenchantment with the practice, Mr Brooks is still a great believer in hand-rearing; in his aviaries, Brown's, Cloncurries and Tasmanians which have been hand-reared have all produced young.

Mr J. Woods - another breeder in Essex - told me how he was warned by his continental suppliers not to allow his pair of Brown's to go to nest early in the year, even if the hen began dropping eggs from the perch. He abided by this advice and did not allow them access to the nest until April; the pair went straight to nest and four young were reared with the hen brooding the young through the entire nestling period.

Derek Simpkin, writing in the *Cage and Aviary Birds Magazine* in nineteen ninety-three, said that his Brown's initially bred in winter, but gradually came around to spring nesting. Heat was required in the nest from the time the young were eight days old, and this was provided by a heating pad fixed in a false bottom of the nest. He recommended heating pads used in wine making; at ten watts they are inexpensive to run and provide a steady temperature of eighty degrees Fahrenheit. He found that rotted wood from willow as a nesting material was a good insulator against cold for early breeders. His birds enjoyed mealworms, which he limited to six per bird per day, boiled corn-on-the-cob daily and a fruit mixture of apple, grapes and pomegranate.

Aggression
Brown's cocks have a reputation for violence towards hens; it is especially difficult to pair a new hen with an old cock that has lost his original established partner, so greater care than usual is needed under such circumstances or the new hen will be killed. The two birds should be housed in adjacent flights until they are accustomed to each other; when introduced, the cock should be placed in the hen's flight so that he is at a slight disadvantage, but if necessary a few of the his inner flight feathers can be clipped or pulled on one wing to slow down his pursuit of the hen. It is best to pair up Brown's when they are still immature, the young pair grow together and incompatibility is then unlikely.

Aviculture in Australia
Hugo Austla lives in northern Western Australia and - amongst other psittacines and finches - maintains a stock of up to sixty Brown's Rosellas, built up over a number of years. Pairs are kept in conventional flights measuring fifteen feet long (4.56m) by four feet wide (1.22m); nest-boxes are used instead of nest-logs, and peat moss as a nest litter has proved to be disliked by the Brown's. In this part of tropical northern Australia, they have a long breeding season, from February right the way through to August, and some of Mr Austla's pairs will manage to rear as many as three nests of young in a season. In southern parts of Australia, breeders find their Brown's going to nest in July and August with activity carrying on into December. The problem in this part of the country is not one of nestlings becoming chilled, but one of nestlings - and eggs - becoming cooked; in October even fledglings have been lost because of excessive heat. Apart from this, the main problem has been the difficulty of making up compatible pairs due to the aggression of cocks towards hens.

According to Mr Austla, the wild Brown's of this area are plentiful and exist in populations which remain in specific areas. Apart from exceptional seasons when rains create temporary water stations in the driest areas, they do not wander far from their safe home base ranges which are chosen simply because of the continued availability of water, and the resulting food supplies and nest sites.

It may be that the partial isolation of populations has lead to a developing of slight colour differences; beside the normal white cheeked nominate race, Mr Austla has stocks of another four distinct types which he is intending to keep in separate strains. Two of these originate from the Kimberley area; the first is the previously described blue cheeked sub-species and the second a type which has the black of the head replaced with dark maroon. Of the other two, one has yellow flecking amongst the red of the head, and one has blue feathers mixed in with the yellow of the breast but lacks the dark edging to the yellow breast feathers.

Colour Varieties
As far as is known, apart from the slight plumage variations already reported, there are no known colour varieties, but I have illustrated my projections of a **Blue** and a **Cinnamon** Brown's Rosella to show how attractive these birds would be.

PENNANT'S or The CRIMSON ROSELLA
Platycercus elegans

Australia: Crimson Rosella, Pennant's Parrakeet, Red Lowry, Mountain Lowry, Julang (Aboriginal).
France: Perruche de Pennant.
Germany: Pennantsittich, or Buschwaldsittich.
Holland: Pennant Rosella.

Length: 14in, 36cm.
Weight: cock 123-169gm, hen 112-146gm.

RESPLENDENT IN ROYAL BLUE and richest crimson with black centred mantle feathers, **Pennant's Rosella** is recognized in three sub-species, *Platycercus elegans elegans*, which is the nominate, *Platycercus elegans melanoptera*, and *Platycercus elegans nigrescens* which is markedly smaller and darker in colour than the other two. In this latter sub-species, the fledglings are maroon-red with a bronze cast and little indication of green, whereas the young of the nominate race are predominantly green with variable patches of crimson spread about their heads and bodies in a haphazard fashion. These two extreme forms used to be clearly recognizable in British stocks, but not any longer, due to indiscriminate cross breeding both completely red and patchy green specimens have long been seen to occur in the same nests; the smaller, darker sub-species seems to have been swallowed up and has disappeared.

Distribution and Feeding Habits
Pennant's is the foremost member of the blue-cheeked group of the Rosella genus; the distribution area of its nominate sub-species - *Platycercus elegans elegans* - spreads in a broad swathe following the coast line from south-east Queensland to south-east South Australia and has been introduced into New Zealand and Norfolk Island; these large parrakeets are resilient against cold wet conditions and are even seen in the snow covered alpine areas of southern Australia - making a spectacular sight.

The smaller **Northern Pennant's Rosella** *(Platycercus elegans nigrescens)* is confined to a coastal strip in the north-east of Queensland which includes areas of tropical rain forest, in complete isolation from its larger relative. The doubtful sub-species **Kangaroo Island Pennant's Rosella** *(Platycercus elegans melanoptera)* is represented by a very small population restricted to Kangaroo Island off the west coast of South Australia and is differentiated only by larger areas of black on feathers of the mantle and back.

Though frequently seen in the gardens and parks of towns and cities in their areas of distribution, these parrakeets generally prefer a forested habitat, where they can be seen feeding both in the trees and at ground level. As well as living off many native species such as eucalyptus, banksia, seeding native conifers and wild figs, they feed on the produce of introduced trees, shrubs and plants - for example: wild rose hips, cotoneaster and pyracantha berries, and seeds of sorrel and clover. From cultivated fruit to seeding heads of introduced scotch thistles, anything remotely digestible seems to be fair game for these rosellas. Like many Australian psittacines, they strip bark and tear open rotten branches in their hunt for termites and wood boring larvae, and search through foliage to find leaves to which the soft bodied psyllid lerps - protected by their crusty shell-like coverings - are attached. Unlike adults, which tend to be seen in pairs or small family groups and have learnt to be wary because of their conspicuous appearance, young Pennant's Rosellas are more reckless, they gather together in larger numbers and are careless in spending much time feeding on open ground.

Description
The cock Pennant's is strikingly coloured with crimson head and body, black mantle feathers edged with crimson, blue and black wings, blackish flights, dark blue central tail feathers, pale blue under-tail tipped with white, and ultramarine cheek patches. He is a only a little bolder in appearance than his equally brilliant hen; she has a smaller head and bill, and a greener wash to the central tail feathers; youngsters attain adult colour at around a year old, but the gloss of full maturity may not be acquired until they are in their third year.

Aviculture in Australia
In the wild, Pennant's commence nesting in October and are still rearing young into January; Australian breeders try to encourage early nesting to avoid youngsters expiring in the heat of their mid-summer. Even so, despite the fact that this parrakeet is arguably the most attractively coloured of its genus, it is so common that aviculturists living within its range often fail to give it aviary space - familiarity leads to a lack of appreciation. In Australia, hand-reared, hand-tame youngsters are popular at first, not just for their looks, but also because they will learn to whistle short tunes, however - once Pennant's are fully mature - fearless pets can become extremely spiteful towards their owners and give nasty bites when being handled.

In Britain, beginners are less likely to purchase Pennant's for inclusion in a mixed collection, but in Australia, novice bird keepers have to be warned against the practice; these large parrakeets have been known to kill even inoffensive ground dwelling species such as quail. So it is not surprising that, in the wild, the smaller Eastern Rosella - which shares most of the Pennant's distribution area - comes off a poor second in the competition for nesting sites against its larger, stronger and more aggressive relative.

Housing
These strong jawed rosellas should be housed in flights covered with welded mesh of not less than sixteen gauge as thin wire can easily be chewed into holes; many escapees have gained their freedom through the aviary roof. Some breeders of the old school stick to the practice of providing flights of thirty feet (9.14m) and even longer for this active and pugnacious species, and it is certainly wise to allow a flight of a minimum length of fifteen (4.57m) to twenty feet (6.09m).

Breeding
If they are well cared for, they can be long lived and productive for many years; there are records of cocks being fertile and helping to raise young well into their twenties, and of hens still breeding in their teens. An English breeder recorded a total of thirty eight young being bred from one hen over a period of thirteen years - not a remarkable yearly average but certainly dependable and consistent. They are mature enough to commence breeding at a year old. Like most Rosellas they can be double brooded, and a few hens can be so eager to get down to a second nest that some breeders advise placing two boxes in the flight to avoid the second clutch of eggs being laid in the same nest as the unfledged young. Feather plucking of young can result if a frustrated hen is eager to go back to nest, and adults which feather bite themselves seem to be more common in Pennant's than any other Rosella. Very little can be more disappointing to its owner than to see a previously gloriously plumaged Pennant's Rosella gradually reducing itself to its fluffy grey underdown.

In Britain, nesting usually commences at the end of April (even later in years of cold springs) and rearing can carry on into late summer and early autumn; soon after, the adults begin to moult - single brooders moult earlier than double brooders. Four to seven eggs is usual but larger clutches are known, and also hens which get into a continuous cycle of egg laying without attempting to sit - a reported twenty-nine eggs in a season could be the record!

Nest-boxes

Advice regarding nest-boxes varies greatly with some breeders recommending 'grandfather clock' nests of four to five feet (1.22m - 1.52m) high by seven to nine inches (178mm - 228mm) square inside, with a deep base of six to eight inches (152mm - 203mm) of nest filler and a nest entrance of three inches (76mm) in diameter; others have been successful with hanging boxes measuring about two feet (.61m) high by seven inches (178mm) square inside, set at an angle of forty five degrees with a slightly smaller tight fitting entrance.

Colour Varieties

Colour varieties in Pennant's Rosellas are a comparatively new development, but the **Blue** - which is an *Autosomal Recessive* - is now well established over the avicultural world. Its effect causes total elimination of psittacin red; crimson areas are changed to greyish white in some strains which possess less melanin, and grey in those strains which are darker. Black areas are retained and blue areas enhanced. Youngsters in immature plumage are much bluer than adults; the reason for which becomes apparent if it is remembered that many normal youngsters have a great deal of green plumage.

A **Cinnamon** variety exists in Australia with blue colour only slightly lighter, and black areas changed to chocolate brown and fawn; a **Cinnamon Blue** could be easily produced.

As far as is known an **Ino** variety does not yet exist in Europe but examples are said to have occurred in Australia; my projection of such a bird shows a Pennant's with blue areas changed to white, black changed to white with tinges of pinkish red in some areas, and crimson changed to light red; eyes will also be red, while feet and bill will be flesh coloured. The variety contemplated is of course not a yellow ground Ino (Lutino), but a red ground Ino - best described as **Rubino**.

The possibility of more than one type of melanin pigment in psittacines is sometimes raised; the strongest indication of this can be seen in one of the latest **Australian Dilute** colour mutations of the Pennant's Rosella, in which the melanin content of black feathers on the back and wings is lacking, reducing them to white, but substantially retained in areas such as cheek patches, wings and lateral tail feathers - giving a strong blue colour. With crimson plumage lightened, the overall effect is a most striking '**Red, White and Blue**' Rosella. Bill, feet and eyes seem little changed from the wild type colour.

This Dilute mutation contrasts strongly with another Dilute variety of questionable origins; the '**Yellow**' **Pennant's** has blue areas on wings, tail and cheeks replaced with a pale bluish white, the back and upper tail are yellowish, the head and body is a mixture of yellow and orange, with orange being concentrated down the centre of the abdomen, vent and on the forehead; feet and bill are flesh coloured and eyes have a plum coloured tint. If this bird were described as a variety of the Adelaide, no question would be raised, but it is a clear fact that a Dilute gene does not change red ground colour to orange and yellow. It would be interesting to examine the young resulting from the pairing of one of these 'Yellows' to a pure wild type bird, if the resulting progeny had any yellow or orange plumage and were different in appearance from a normal Pennant's Rosella, the conclusion would obviously be that the 'Yellow' was itself not a Pennant's.

In nineteen ninety-three an English breeder sent me photographs of a young Pennant's with orange plumage; it reverted to crimson through the autumn and winter as it moulted out. The same breeder sent me more photographs in nineteen ninety-four of two Pennant's he had obtained; an adult hen had deep blue spread over the lower abdomen, and her son had a ragged ridge of blue spreading from the throat down the centre of the breast to the belly. The birds appear to be pure Pennant's, and not adulterated with Mealy blood. Initial breeding results suggest that the **Blue-bellied** mutant is extremely dominant, which might raise alarm in some quarters, in case the wild type stood in some danger of becoming swamped.

The ADELAIDE ROSELLA
Platycercus adelaidae

Australia: Adelaide Rosella, Adelaide Parrakeet, or Pheasant Parrakeet.
France: Perruche Adelaide.
Germany: Adelaidesittich.
Holland: Adelaide Rosella.

Length: $13^3/_4$in, 35cm.
Weight: cock 112-165gm, hen 100-160gm.

SPLIT INTO TWO SUB-SPECIES, the nominate form of the **Adelaide Rosella**, *(Platycercus adelaidae adelaidae)*, is a deeper and more even orange throughout its head and underparts than *Platycercus adelaidae subadelaidae*; birds of this latter type are of a buffish orange-yellow in equivalent areas of plumage, with darker orange flecks. Indiscriminate cross-breeding within aviculture between the two sub-species has caused a merging, with the outcome proving detrimental to the more red-orange nominate race.

Hybridization
The Adelaide shows its close affinity to the Pennant's by its general size, form, colour pattern and habits. Cross breeding Yellow Rosellas with Pennant's produces hybrids similar to the lighter sub-species of Adelaide, and this has been done with frequency in Britain in the past when Yellow Rosella hens were in short supply. So, there is no way of knowing for sure if the available Adelaides are in fact hybrids or descendants of such hybrids. To compound the problem, surplus Yellow Rosella cocks have also been paired to Adelaide hens, or hybrid hens, resulting in birds part way between Adelaides and Yellow Rosellas. With continuous selection, hybrids with less red-orange have been produced resulting in the buff coloured 'Yellow Rosellas' of today - which unfortunately predominate and are increasing in number above the pure Yellow Rosellas.

Distribution
There is also a question over the viability of the Adelaide as a separate species or even sub-species, with suggestions that the populations of these Rosellas are established wild natural hybrids between the Pennant's and Yellow Rosellas; of the two separate populations those of the northern area consist of *Platycercus adelaidae subadelaidae*, while the southern birds are made up of the darker red orange race and a smattering of paler birds. However, it is reported that the red-orange Adelaides wander into the territory of the Yellow Rosella and it could be surmised that these paler specimens are in fact of recent hybrid origin coming from specimens of the nominate red-orange race of Adelaide mating with the Yellow Rosella. Immature Adelaides are predominantly green - another similarity with Pennant's - with orange patches on head and body.

A questionable sub-species *(Platycercus adelaidae fleurensis)*, which is more brick red in colour, comes from the Fleurieu Peninsula, South Australia - a clue to the possible reason for the colour of this race is gleaned by noting that just off the point of this peninsula lies Kangaroo Island - the home of the Pennant's Rosella sub-species *Platycercus elegans melanoptera*. The population of the nominate race spreads outwards from the South Australian city of Adelaide itself into the forested valleys of the Mount Lofty Ranges, while the paler sub-species - *Platycercus adelaidae subadelaidae* - lives northwards along tree lined water courses of valleys of the southern Flinders Ranges.

Colour Varieties

The **Lutino** is a very rare colour variety in the Adelaide and said to be an *Autosomal Recessive* in its inheritance. The Ino effect causes total lack of melanin, leaving yellow, cream and white plumage marked with orange and red; the bill and feet are flesh coloured while eyes are vivid red.

The **Cinnamon** is being established in Australia and its effect changes melanin black to melanin brown, black areas (especially on the mantle) become brown and fawn, creating a predominantly light brown and orange parrakeet which is very attractive - it is a *Sex-linked Recessive* in its inheritance.

A **Blue** variety of the Adelaide would be rather pointless, being practically indistinguishable in appearance from Blue Pennant's. I sincerely hope that no future breeders attempt introducing the Blue - or any other varieties for that matter - into the Adelaide via the Pennant's. Indiscriminate hybridization between the Pennant's, Adelaide, and Yellow Rosella has caused enough confusion as it is.

HAWTHORN BERRIES *(below)* are enjoyed by the Rosellas, the largest species can crack open the small, hard stones at their centres and extricate the kernels.

THE LUTINO ADELAIDE *(right)* is an exceptional avicultural beauty and still an extreme rarity at present; the most famous example is that owned by Stan Sindel of New South Wales.

The YELLOW or YELLOW-RUMPED ROSELLA
Platycercus flaveolus

Australia: Yellow Rosella, Yellow Parrot, Yellow-rumped Parrot, Swamp Lowry, Murray Smoker, Murrumbidgee Rosella, or River Rosella.
France: Perruche à couleur de paille.
Germany: Strohsittich, or Strohgelber Plattschweifsittich.
Holland: Strogele Rosella.

Length: $13^1/_2$in, 34cm.
Weight: cock 110-135gm, hen 105-117gm.

THE MOST CHOICE EXAMPLES of the **Yellow Rosella** *(Platycercus flaveolus)* - less well known as the Straw or Yellow-rumped Rosella - are considered to be those with a clear lemon yellow colour over heads and underparts. Once again, this species follows the general stamp and pattern of the Pennant's and the Adelaide - it also has the typical blue cheek patches. Apart from a band of red on the forehead and the fact that hens may have a slight orange tinge below the bill, there should be no extensive spread of orange, but nowadays many birds offered for sale as 'Yellow Rosellas' often have the appearance of the lighter form of the Adelaide.

Hybridization has lead to the pure and extreme examples of the species becoming rare; adulteration with Adelaide blood creates a 'brassy' buff coloured bird with orange suffusion. Crossing the Yellow Rosella with the Pennant's produces young which are indistinguishable from Adelaides of the sub-species *Platycercus adelaidae subadelaidae.*

Breeding
Yellow Rosellas are not always as free breeding as many of the commoner species of their genus, and sometimes miss a season without making an attempt at nesting. This usually happens when spring weather turns dry and cold, when the parrakeets can easily slip into an early moult. Mild showery weather brings them into breeding condition and then they are quite capable of rearing two broods by the end of the summer. As a general rule, even young birds are easily sexed by the cock's larger head and bill and cleaner colour, but some hens are quite outstanding and difficult to distinguish from cocks.

Adult cock Yellow Rosellas can persecute their mates and be savage towards them, even out of the breeding season, so a few secondary feathers may need removing from one wing at these times to slow the cock's pursuit. The feathers can be cut or pulled; if pulled they will be grown again in a few weeks, by which time the pair may have settled down to a more amicable life; if cut they will not be replaced until the end of season moult. Highly active and pugnacious birds such as these must not be set up in cramped accommodation; a roomy flight of around twenty feet (6.09m) long, three feet (.91m) wide and six feet (1.83m) high will help to prevent potentially dangerous incidents.

As with the other Rosellas, one indication of an imminent attack against another bird is the action of tucking in the bill and advancing with obvious intent towards their target; a rapid shivering of the wings may be seen in both shows of aggression and courtship; other typical actions include tail wagging, strutting and short clear musical calls - more accentuated on the part of the cock. In Britain, courtship and nesting usually begins in spring as late as the month of May.

Nervous hens are common in this species, and sudden loud noises, or the cock's alarm calls, can easily draw such hens off the nest with a too persistent regularity.

Habitat

Yellow Rosellas are perfectly hardy in our climate, despite having originated from a homeland where summer temperatures are frequently at levels we would never ever experience here in Britain. In the summer heat of their wild home these Rosellas retire to rest in the foliage of eucalyptus and red gum, their colour patterns being a perfect camouflage as they sit and doze. These tree species are common along the banks of the inland systems of Murray, Darling, Lachlan and Murrumbidgee rivers - the Yellow Rosellas' chosen habitat along the water courses of south eastern Australia. Though they may venture into drier areas of scrub or mallee, the birds feel safer in these river bordering trees, and return to them to feed in their branches, to roost, take shelter, and excavate their nest hollows. In times of partial drought, cultivated farm land - with its man made irrigation systems - acts as a welcome safety net.

Colour Varieties

There is a **Dilute ('Yellow')** variety being established in Australia which is an *Autosomal Recessive,* its effect is to cause partial to almost complete lack of melanin, making yellow plumage more pure in colour, reducing the black on mantle feathers to pale grey-fawn, making cheek patches and blue on wings a pale silvery blue, but retaining and clarifying the red frontal band.

In my own strain of Yellow Rosellas, built up around twenty years ago, a specimen appeared with a few yellowish white feathers in the flights and tail, but slightly pied specimens such as this are also known in Australia and this does not seem to be a very useful variety to develop in this species. A **Blue** variety is not known to exist but my projection of the appearance of such a bird shows an example very similar to a Blue Pennant but with yellow areas replaced by silvery white instead of grey. Neither is a Lutino known to exist; but a projection of a **Lutino** Yellow Rosella of the purest form shows a lemon yellow parrakeet with white cheeks, white on wings and tail, red frontal band, flesh coloured bill and feet, and red eyes.

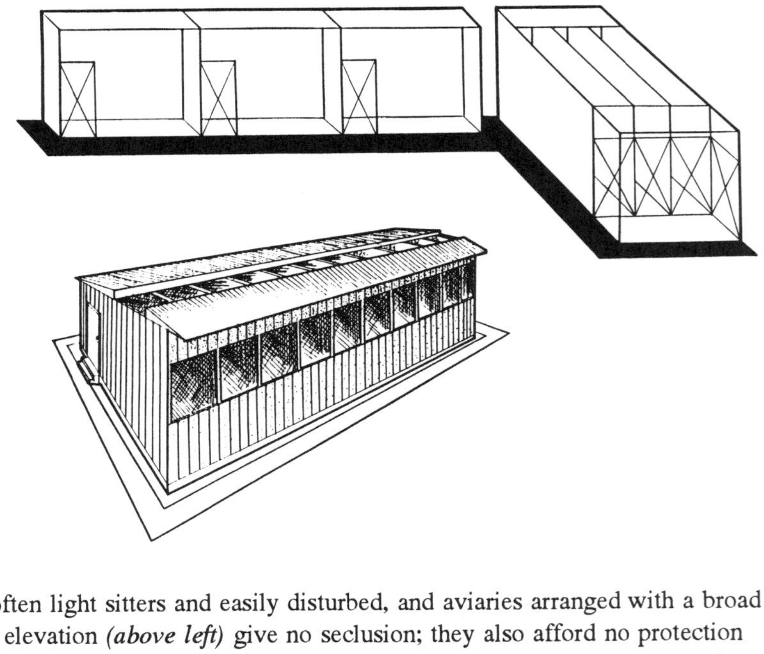

YELLOW ROSELLA HENS are often light sitters and easily disturbed, and aviaries arranged with a broad expanse of wire mesh on the front elevation *(above left)* give no seclusion; they also afford no protection from predators and prevent birds retiring to a comfortable distance from the observer; flights arranged length ways *(above right)* with a wire mesh covered front walk-way overcome these problems. The row of flights *(bottom)* gives good protection against the elements and predators with its partly boarded and double wired front elevation; the feeding corridor is situated at the back, and the partial roofing of translucent sheeting affords plenty of light for the occupants.

The TASMANIAN, GREEN or YELLOW-BELLIED ROSELLA
Platycercus caledonicus

Australia: Tasmanian Rosella, Green Rosella, Yellow-bellied Rosella, Caledonian Rosella, or Mountain Rosella.
France: Perruche à ventre jaune.
Germany: Gelbbauchsittich, Gelbbäuchiger Plattschweifsittich.
Holland: Geelbuik Rosella.

Length: 14$^1/_2$in, 37cm.
Weight: cock 105-165gm, hen 90-130gm.

NOWADAYS WELL ESTABLISHED in Europe, some examples of the **Tasmanian (or Green) Rosella** *(Platycercus caledonicus)* show evidence of cross-breeding with the Yellow Rosella, which - to the uninitiated - it superficially resembles. However, there are marked differences in plumage colour, as described below, and there is also a great difference in size and build. The Tasmanian Rosella is a stout, thick set parrakeet, the largest member of the genus, so one way of distinguishing Tasmanian x Yellow Rosella hybrids is by their much smaller size. In the 'sixties and 'seventies hybridization with Pennant's - presumably to retain at least some characteristics of a dwindling species - resulted in strains which showed heavy red flecking; but, despite this previous hybridization with closely related species, pure bred birds can still be found.

Appearance of Pure Bred Tasmanians

The tail - with dark green central feathers and blue lateral feathers tipped whitish - is in keeping with the appearance of the rest of the group; as also are the ultramarine edging, blackish patch on the wing, and dark blue flights. The blue cheek patches give evidence of this parrakeet's close affinity with the Pennant-Adelaide-Yellow Rosella group. Its yellow head, breast, belly and under-tail coverts, as well as the red frontal band over the bill, are characteristics shared with the Yellow Rosella. However, in contrast with the yellow rump of this smaller species, the Tasmanian has a dark green rump, with a paler golden-green or orange-green edging to each feather; also, the centres of the mantle feathers are a less intense black, their edges are green instead of yellow, and much narrower than those of the other members of this group. Hens are markedly smaller in the head and bill, and tend to show far more orange flecking around the head, throat (even the breast in some specimens) as well as the vent feathers. Immatures are much greener overall and do not acquire adult coloration until well into their second year.

Though not mentioned by Joseph Forshaw in either of his standard works, *'Parrots of the World'* or *'Australian Parrots'*, Dr Groen (in his popular work *'Australian Parrakeets')* writes of an overall difference in colour between birds from eastern Tasmania and those from the colder and damper western side, with the former type being 'brighter'; other writers seem to have picked up this reference. Certainly there are similar differences in individual Tasmanians which run parallel to differences in the Yellow Rosella, and these are brought about by one factor - the extent of red suffusion. Birds with that basic 'brassy' yellow colour, and orange flecking and suffusion on sides of the head, throat and under-tail coverts are far commoner in aviculture than those possessing a pure lemon yellow colour with just a minimum of orange suffusion around the eye and on the under-tail coverts. These paler birds - which I think are far more desirable - have a bluish green edging to the mantle feathers whereas the 'brassy' Tasmanians show edgings with some orange suffusion.

In the Wild

The Tasmanian Rosella is plentiful, even common in some parts of its natural homeland of Tasmania, the surrounding islands, and the larger islands of Bass Strait. Its scientific name indicates its origin as the island of New Caledonia, a strange mistake by biologists of the late eighteenth century, which has never been corrected. The Tasmanian is thought to be the most ancient of all the Rosellas and is closer to the ancestral stock than any others of the genus.

Out of the nesting season during the Tasmanian winter, they can be seen in small groups and even flocks; they visit farms and farmland searching for gleanings, and are even seen in populated areas; however, once the nesting instinct becomes strong - nesting takes place from November to February - breeding pairs retire to wooded and forested land. Hollow trunks and limbs of eucalypts are the favourite nesting sites, but they have even been found to nest in rock crevices and old remote abandoned buildings. These hardy birds range into the mountains and snow covered alpine areas, but avoid moorland and other bleak regions entirely devoid of trees. Forshaw mentions the report of an exceptional occurrence at the end of the last century when thousands of these Rosellas suddenly appeared in the south of the island; his inference seems to be that great numbers were driven from their seasonal haunts by extreme weather; an influx of such proportions has - so far as is known - not been described in recent times. Though a protected species, farmers destroy them as pests under licence because of their depredations in orchards; otherwise they live on the wide variety of available wild fruits, seeds, grasses, berries, blossoms, shoots and buds, as well as larvae, pupae and insects. As in England, introduced hawthorn is widely used for hedges on Tasmanian farm land, and its berries are favoured by the parrakeets, as are the buds of the introduced basket willow.

The Tasmanian Rosella is not present naturally on Australia itself, and is scarce there as an aviary subject. Taking the fact into account that it is suited to cooler climes, it is not surprising that Australian aviculturists in northern mainland areas have difficulties in keeping and breeding this species. Their lateness in going to nest means that hens are incubating and young are in the nest at the very hottest time of year, resulting in desertions of eggs and deaths of nestlings. Cool, shady, well protected areas for aviaries and nests are imperative for success, and aviary sprinkler systems are recommended to help the birds cool down.

In British Aviaries

This parrakeet's method of flight is more direct, less swooping and gliding than its relatives; it is more prone to obesity than the other Rosellas and needs a long flight to provide plenty of exercise in order to combat this serious problem, which often prevents successful breeding. Bachelor cocks left on their own for several years will become very aggressive and are likely to kill any hens suddenly introduced into their territory; introduction of new partners should be done gradually and with caution. The aggressiveness of cocks frequently leads to infertile eggs as frightened hens avoid their continual pursuit by hiding in the nest; starvation can also result under these extreme circumstances. With well suited pairs, both cock and hen will commence the usual tail wagging display, and the cock will regurgitate food for his hen from around the middle of April, with initial matings taking place later in the month. Both partners make quiet musical calls to each other which can only be heard by an observer standing close by. Hen Tasmanians usually commence laying from the beginning of May to the beginning of June, double brooding is known with second nests of eggs being produced as early as July - if a second nest-box is provided - so that the last young fledge in September. Damaged parrakeets should not be written off as breeders: even though it had only a third to a quarter of its upper mandible left after being attacked through the wire by a cock Twenty-eight, an English breeder's hen Tasmanian still proved able to rear its own young.

Apart from the possibility of a **Cinnamon** mutation being established in Australia, colour varieties seem to be unknown.

The STANLEY or WESTERN ROSELLA
Platycercus icterotis

Australia: Western Rosella, Stanley Rosella, Stanley Parrakeet, Yellow-cheeked Rosella, or Goodt-un-goodt (Aboriginal).
France: Perruche de Stanley.
Germany: Stanleysittich, Gelbbäckiger Plattschweifsittich, Gelbwangenrosella, or Scharlachsittich.
Holland: Stanley Rosella.

Length: $10^1/_2$in, 27cm.
Weight: cock 59-80gm, hen 52-71gm.

ORIGINATING FROM the south-western corner of Western Australia, the **Stanley** or **Western Rosella** is the smallest of the genus *Platycercus* - it has also been more grandly named as *'the Earl of Derby Parrakeet'*. The cock is mainly scarlet throughout its head and body with large golden yellow cheek patches. It is the only Rosella to show clear sexual dimorphism in its plumage; hens are variable, but in all cases much duller than cocks with more green about their upper breast and head - their cheek patches have only broken areas of yellow.

Two sub-species exist which in their extreme forms are very different in appearance; *Platycercus icterotis icterotis* from coastal areas - the greener nominate race known to Australian bird breeders as the **'Green-backed'** - and the sub-species *Platycercus icterotis xanthogenys* from dry inland areas, which, because of extensive red edging to the mantle feathers, is known in Australia as the **'Red-backed'**.

Appearance

Cocks of the nominate race have the head, breast, belly, vent and under-tail coverts coloured scarlet, with flecks of green on the flanks and vent area - feathers of breast and belly have faint dark edges. The feathers of the mantle, scapulars and tertials are blackish at their very centres, edged green and variably tipped with red in the mantle area, the rump feathers are dark green with maroon tipping, central tail feathers are green; lateral tail feathers are dark blue at their bases, shading to pale blue and finally whitish at their tips; the under-tail is sky blue. The characteristic black band of the Rosellas is present on the upper wing followed by dark blue on the outer wing, the primaries are blackish lined with blue on their outer edges. The large flaring cheek patches are brilliant yellow, the irides are dark brown, bill pale grey and feet brown-grey.

In the most extreme examples of cocks of the Red-backed sub-species, the cheeks are a very pale whitish yellow, and the bright green areas of the nominate sub-species are replaced by greyish olive. Mantle feathers can be edged entirely with red, and the maroon tips to the rump feathers are wider and lighter red. The central tail feathers are greyish olive, edged and tipped with dark blue. Hens of this type have the same colour differences in line with those of their cocks, but with broken areas of colour on cheeks and body, in keeping with hens of the nominate form.

In Britain, during the nineteen sixties, both races were being bred and could easily be distinguished, but nowadays the delineations of the two separate forms are seldom seen; imports from the continent of a small type of Green-backed Stanley in the late 'sixties - because of their prolific nature - soon caused a predominance of this strain in Britain, and this was detrimental to the increase in numbers of the Red-backed. Selective breeding with birds which show a tendency towards Red-backed visual characteristics could help to reinstate these attractive inland Stanleys.

Despite large numbers being bred through their tendency to produce two good broods per season, a great many youngsters used to be lost in the autumn of the year due to their susceptibility to internal worms. Once de-worming became a matter of course in Britain, the number of Stanleys rapidly increased, with the only possible set back for breeders being a tendency for a disproportionately larger number of cocks to be produced.

Despite their susceptibility to internal parasites, the powers of recovery after serious physical damage are often demonstrated by the Stanley and the other Rosellas; I remember in particular one young Stanley cock which, on fledging, had collided with a corner post of the aviary. His chest was split right the way down so that, as he breathed, the two sides of his breast opened and closed to reveal the white keel bone. Gradually the wound began to heal but by then the jutting breast bone was preventing the gash from closing; instinctively the little fledgling parrakeet gnawed this bone away until it was level with the flesh, allowing healing to become complete. This same bird was completely tame as a youngster because of the continual handling and hand feeding needed to help him survive; he learnt to pipe little tunes. Though a great little character, once he became adult he was totally useless for breeding purposes as his tameness had developed into a fearless aggression against any prospective mate; he would also attack me when I entered his aviary; finally he picked a fight through the wire with a large cock Eastern Rosella and had his upper mandible almost torn off, but again survived - though with his bill twisted to one side.

The dull coloured nestling Stanleys moult into a transitional plumage in the early autumn, with the resulting brick red colouring of the young cocks not being replaced by scarlet till the following year; even so, year old birds in transitional plumage are just as likely to breed successfully as fully coloured adults. It has been known for pairs in which the partners have been placed together for a period of only three or four weeks to produce fertile eggs and rear young, however, it is much better to introduce the prospective partners in the autumn preceding the spring breeding season so that they are thoroughly accustomed to each other.

Nesting Season

In Australia, the Stanley's nesting season commences between August and September, but here in Britain nesting begins from the end of April to the first days of May, with second nests being started from the end of June to the beginning of July. In Australia, young are known to spend as little as four weeks in the nest in the warmest areas of the country; in Britain, they grow at a slower pace and take almost five weeks to fledge - because of our cooler climate.

Of all the Rosellas, the Stanley - having developed in isolation - is the species showing closest affinities with members of the genus *Psephotus*, especially the Redrump *(Psephotus haematonotus)* and the Manycolour *(Psephotus varius)*, with which it shares characteristics of sexual dimorphism, and similarities of flight, behaviour and calls.

Chosen Habitat in the Wild

The Stanley prefers scrub, grassland, open woodland, trees edging water, orchards, and cultivated land; the birds are regularly seen fearlessly feeding on grain spillage around farm buildings and paddocks; the species has benefited from the spread of agriculture, but is held back from greater increase in its numbers by the competition of the larger, stronger and more numerous Twenty-eight Parrakeet.

The birds feed predominantly on seeding plants and grasses, but also take berries, buds, fruit, blossom, nectar and insects. Though a protected species, they are sometimes a nuisance in orchards and as a result can be persecuted by fruit growers; in some areas, farmers are allowed to destroy them when they are found feeding on crops.

Colour Varieties

Both a **Blue** and a **Lutino** mutation of the Stanley have occurred. In nineteen eighty-seven I received a message from the late Sid Gale in New South Wales, advising that he was going to see a Blue Stanley and would let me know if he was successful in purchasing it; sadly, the next message received from Australia was to tell me of Sid's sudden death.

Having no description or photograph to guide me, I made a projected painting of a cock and hen Blue Stanley, as well as a pair of Lutinos; some four years later I was pleased to see photographs of a Blue Stanley cock in an Australian publication which proved my projection to be correct. Povl Jorgensen - current expert on parrots for the Danish bird societies' magazine *'Dansk Fuglehold'* - told me of seeing Blue Stanleys at the aviaries of a German mutation specialist. In the Blue, all scarlet areas are reduced to pale silvery grey, yellow to white, greens to various tones of peacock blue; the black wing patch is of course retained, and the adjoining blue on the wing is enhanced and shown to be of an ultramarine shade.

The cock Lutino Stanley is a spectacular bird, with scarlet areas made even more vivid, green areas altered to brilliant yellow, blue and black areas changed to white, eyes are red, and bill and feet flesh coloured; the hen has variegated areas of yellow interspersed with the scarlet of the upper breast and head. It is reported that both these varieties are in the early stages of being established in Australia. As far as I know, no Blues or Lutinos have yet appeared in Britain, and the first breeder here to be lucky enough to have the first opportunity of establishing such rare mutation Stanleys will have won a great prize.

IN A ROSELLA COLLECTION (here, two pairs each of Mealies, Pennant's and Stanleys), the Stanleys provide an additional 'buffer' between the more aggressive species in conjunction with docile parrakeets like Barraband's, Bourke's and Plum-headeds - used as separators to prevent disruption to nesting.

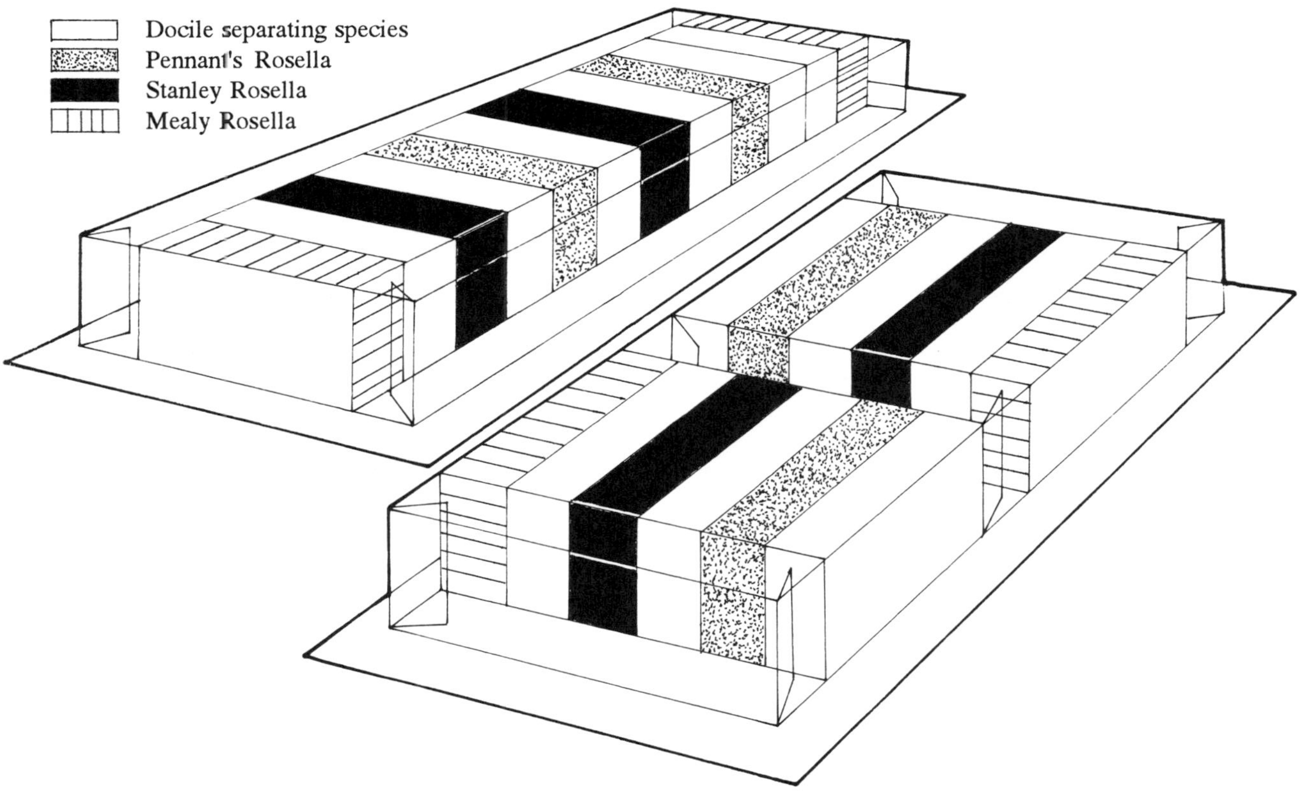

TERRACE AVIARIES *(top)* with mesh covered feeding alley at back and service/safety alley.
AVIARY BLOCK *(bottom)* with central feeding alley and service/safety alleys both ends.

THE MEMBERS OF BARNARDIUS have very similar physical characteristics, personalities, habits and calls to the Rosella species, which - in general - they supersede in the more arid interior. They differ markedly from the Rosellas in the coloration of their plumage, especially because of the conspicuous yellow band across the backs of their necks - a mutual feature of this group of sturdy parrakeets - which has caused them to be known by Australian bird keepers as *'Ringneck Parrots'*; in conversation, this sometimes causes confusion with European breeders who only refer to the Asiatic/African *Psittacula* species as *'Ringneck'*. In addition, their bills are slightly wider, heavier and more notched than the Rosellas and there is said to be a difference in the construction of the skull in the region of the ear.

Though most adult hen Barnard's and Cloncurries show the underwing stripe, only some adult hens possess this stripe in the Port Lincoln and Twenty-eight, and - though all adult cocks of the genus entirely lack the feature - it is often present in immatures of both sexes of the Barnard's and Cloncurry; it is present in immature hens of the Port Lincoln and the Twenty-eight, but usually missing in young cocks of both these types.

The birds from eastern Australia (Barnard's and Cloncurries) lack the black heads of the birds from the west (Port Lincolns and Twenty-eights) but intermediate types do exist through hybridization where the central Australian distribution areas of the two forms encroach upon one another.

In the late nineteen-sixties and nineteen-seventies, all members of the genus *Barnardius* were scarce and in high demand by British and European aviculturists, and competition for the acquisition of these desirable parrakeets pushed the prices up and up. Breeders from the continent were regular visitors to England, searching for Port Lincolns, Twenty-eights and Cloncurries - the latter being the most expensive and commanding as much as £3,000 per pair, a large amount of cash for those days.

Many English breeders of that time found the whole of the genus difficult subjects to breed; the main problem - apart from sexing - seeming to have been the birds' preference to go to nest very early in the year when the days were shortest and the weather at its worst. All four are much more easily obtainable in the nineteen-nineties and many breeders throughout Europe have the pleasure of savouring success in the form of nests of newly fledged youngsters.

2. *The Species and Sub-species of Genus Barnardius*

BARNARD'S PARRAKEET
Barnardius barnardi

Australia: Mallee Ringneck Parrot, Scrub Parrot, Bula Bula or Buln Buln.
France: Perruche Barnard.
Germany: Barnardsittich.
Holland: Barnard Parkiet.

Length: $13^3/_4$in. 35cm.
Weight: cock 114-143gm, hen 105-138gm.

LUMINOUS SHADES of turquoise green and ultramarine are the most striking colours in the breast, head, and wing plumage of a cock **Barnard's Parrakeet** *(Barnardius barnardi)* in perfect condition, and these are enhanced by a broad yellow collar at the hind neck, a bluish wash over the fore part of the cheeks, a blue-black mantle, yellow-green bands blended across the mid wing coverts, a broad jagged band of yellow mottled with orange across the abdomen, and a band of red just above the cere. His rump is green, central tail feathers dark green above and shaded with blue, lateral tail feathers are pale blue tipped whitish, like the Rosellas', as also are the flights which are blackish edged with ultramarine. His irides are dark brown, bill pale grey and feet brown-grey - also as the Rosellas.

Cocks can be distinguished from their mates by the deep blue-black on their mantles and backs, and their slightly more brilliant colour in general; hens are marginally slighter in their build and have greenish mantles and backs, otherwise the sexes are much alike.

Distribution and Habits in the Wild

The Barnard's is reasonably common, but less so than in former times in the vicinities of some places where human settlements and farm lands have lead to the depletion of the species preferred habitat - that of mallee (a type of gum, but also used to describe a habitat of scrub land with low growing eucalyptus), and lightly wooded areas adjacent to tree lined waterways. The iridescent plumage of this parrakeet makes it particularly striking when seen in its native sandy habitat.

The nominate form of Barnard's *(Barnardius barnardi barnardi)* is widespread across its inland territory, covering areas of eastern South Australia and north west Victoria through western New South Wales and on into southern Queensland.

Argument seems to exist as to whether other regional races of the species, which differ slightly in shades of colour and size, should be regarded as sub-species or could even be the result of hybridization with the Port Lincoln, but three are recognized, including the nominate type. The most distinctive is the Cloncurry Parrakeet *(Barnardius barnardi macgillivrayi)* which is the most northerly form and lives in an isolated distribution area. The third sub-species *(Barnardius barnardi whitei)*, which has an indistinct range seeming to be on the western fringe of the nominate's distribution area, with which it merges, differs in being slightly smaller than the nominate and in having a lighter, greener back and mantle, with the iridescent shades of turquoise subdued to a more yellowish green.

Though found in other situations, Barnard's are most often seen in areas of mallee woodland, and in Australia are known as *'Mallee Ringnecks'*. They feed on the ground in the open, off seeding grasses and other plants, and - as heat builds through the day - retire to feed in the shade of trees, or seek shelter from the sun deep amongst their foliage; the various sorts of eucalyptus are their preferred foraging stations for blossoms, seeds and fruits. Barnard's do not show a nomadic disposition, but tend to stay around their home area, unless weather conditions and lack of food forces them to seek provisions further abroad.

Unless drought conditions persist, in their native land, Barnard's Parrakeets commence nesting activity in August and continue through into January.

Their unobtrusive single note whistling calls are softer in comparison with the Port Lincoln and delivered with a deliberate rhythm, but when disturbed or frightened they give a louder rapid alarm call - like the Rosellas; and they also have their close relatives' same swooping flight, with spreading tail as they alight on the perch.

Nesting in British Aviaries

After fixing the attention of his hen by calling, and flying rapidly and repeatedly up and down the length of the aviary, the cock settles along side her and begins his courtship display, which is very similar to that of the Rosellas; with an excited chattering and a crouching stance he flares his tail and wags it rapidly from side to side, jutting and vibrating his shoulders as he does so; if the hen does not back away in apprehension but is in a matching state of breeding condition, this performance impresses her enough to accept his offers of regurgitated food, after which the flurry of mating may follow.

Some individual specimens are happier with a shallow hanging nest-box, but some breeders find their birds prefer really deep nests - three to four feet deep (.91m - 1.22m) - with a roomy interior of nine to ten inches square inside (228mm - 225mm). The nest may be set at an angle of thirty to forty-five degrees from the vertical to prevent hens dropping straight onto their eggs, and should be protected with overhead cover as - when placed in the sun - excessive heat can cause hens to desert. The entrance needs to be quite snug at two and a half inches in diameter (65mm), and in any case the birds will gnaw away around the hole to suit their own requirements. It is usual to leave nest-boxes in position the year round, because it is likely the birds will miss the season entirely if they are discouraged from nesting early.

These parrakeets may need to be three or four years old before serious breeding attempts are made. Barnard's are usually early breeders, and hens will start working the nest for months - from as early as Christmas - before actually going to nest. Cocks have been seen feeding and mating with their hens as early as January, with mating even taking place on the floor, but hens are not always so receptive, and if both members of the pair do not come into condition at the same time the season is wasted.

Trouble can ensue when the hen has come into condition before the cock, and then loses her enthusiasm before the cock gains his; when he comes into full condition he is likely to persecute and attack her if she shows no positive response to his advances. If the cock and hen are totally incompatible, there may be no alternative but to provide new partners and hope that these may be accepted.

If held back until the spring and the weather turns suddenly warm and dry, such early breeders as Barnard's can easily miss a season by dropping into the moult, and interest can even be lost completely by April. If the birds have not started to moult, the presentation of one or more different types of nest may stimulate interest. If the hen begins to stay in the nest at night, this is a sign that she will soon commence laying.

Barnard's are not as easy to breed in comparison with the commoner Rosellas, their owner's choice of a mate is not always theirs and if a pair are incompatible a great deal of time can be lost; because of this, the acquisition of fully adult unpaired birds is less favoured than obtaining a young pair which are more likely to pair bond as they mature and grow together; purchasing a small group of youngsters and allowing them to select their own mates, is another alternative.

They do not take kindly to interference when nesting, and a too curious attendant can easily ruin the birds' nesting attempts and cause desertion; sudden changes made to their surroundings or routine, or the birds of neighbouring flights being moved around will have the same detrimental effect. Even so, double brooding is also a possibility with a good established pair.

The usual clutch of eggs is four to six, and the incubation period can be slightly longer than that of the Rosellas at around twenty days, with the young remaining in the nest between five and six weeks - depending on the weather and depth of box. The fledglings are independent of their parents after a couple of weeks, and are duller in colour with mature adult plumage being attained from between a year to eighteen months old.

In Australia, Barnard's are popular as pets because of their ability to whistle short tunes, but they are less favoured as aviary birds because they are too aggressive in a communal flight, and too common in their own country for individual pairs to be afforded their own aviaries, when rarer species are available and need the space. Hand-reared specimens are very aggressive, especially when breeding, and will attack their owners at feeding time or if the nest is approached.

Colour Varieties

Beautiful colour varieties of *Barnardius* species are in existence: in the Barnard's itself a **Blue** variety is becoming established, with yellow and orange changing to white, and green areas to skyblue, cobalt and ultramarine. Less striking is a **Pied** variety with colours made paler over the upper parts and yellow spreading over the head, breast and belly.

LOW GROWING EUCALYPTUS and scrub, typical of one of Barnard's Parrakeet's chosen habitats.

The CLONCURRY PARRAKEET
Barnardius barnardi macgillivrayi

Australia: Cloncurry Parrot, or Macgillivray's Collared Parrot.
France: Perruche Cloncurry.
Germany: Cloncurrysittich.
Holland: Cloncurry Parkiet.

Length: 13in, 33cm.
Weight: cock 120-128gm, hen 99-106gm.

PROBABLY THE FIRST to gain success with the **Cloncurry Parrakeet** *(Barnardius barnardi macgillivrayi)* in England was the late Ron Godwin of Cheltenham, a man well remembered for his enthusiasm and pride for the rare parrakeets - rare for those days - that he kept and bred, he is the person that first comes to mind whenever I see these birds. They also remind me of Cotswold parrot breeder Alan Oliver, who has long been an enthusiast of this attractive bird; it is one parrakeet that he remembers as being highly priced and beyond the reach of all but the wealthiest breeders in the nineteen-sixties; these memories heighten the pleasure he gets nowadays from his own breeding of Cloncurry Parrakeets.

Some specimens nowadays show the unfortunate mark of being hybridized with Barnard's in their darker green feathering, but the birds in Alan's collection are the pale pastel colours that they should be, and possess a great luminosity in their plumage.

Unlike other *Barnardius* species - Twenty-eights and Port Lincolns - the smaller Cloncurry has not been found to be destructive to the fabric of Alan's aviaries, but they do need plenty of space, being active and swift flying aviary occupants. Contrary to the usual nature of broadtail parrakeets, Alan has not found cocks to be pugnacious towards their hens; fertility and hatchability has been high and, though they would go down as soon as January if encouraged, they are quite willing to wait until the middle of March and will get on with the job irrespective of good or bad weather.

Heads of dandelions and groundsel, as well as seeding chickweed, are eagerly sought by the parents when rearing their young. Along with the usual parrakeet seed mixture, apple is fed regularly and at breeding time the diet is supplemented with *'Haith's Nectarblend', 'Haith's Rearing and Condition food', 'PTX'* and a sprinkle of *'SA37' (Intervet)* - which is a vitamin/mineral powder frequently used by bird breeders.

Appearance
The differences in appearance between the Cloncurry and Barnard's Parrakeet would seem to be sufficient for it to be considered a species in its own right, but this is not so and the former is regarded as a sub-species of the latter. The Cloncurry is a smaller bird than Barnard's and - though it still has the blackish flights shaded with deep blue - the rest of the dark shades of the nominate's plumage are reduced considerably, so that the predominant colours are light green with a strong turquoise tint (especially over the head and across the back), pale blue (on the cheeks, wings and under surface of the tail) and a pale lemon yellow (on the collar, lower breast and upper belly), though a pale orange dappling still occurs across the breast/belly area, and this yellow 'stomacher' is very much broader than it is in the Barnard's.

The broad red frontal band of the nominate form is missing in the Cloncurry, but there is a trace of a pale yellow-fawn indefinable colour beneath the turquoise just over the cere; youngsters sometimes have a more definite pale orange in this area which is soon moulted out. Hens are slightly smaller in the head and bill and usually (but not always) a little less bright in their colours; cocks have flatter, broader heads - but they are not always easy to sex.

Distribution and Habits in the Wild

Like its larger relative, the Cloncurry favours living amongst eucalyptus trees, not just for the sake of the food and shelter but also for the nesting sites they provide; the sub-species is most often seen where the eucalypts follow the courses of rivers. It is greatly dependent and gains most benefit from the blossom, fruit and seeds produced along this riverine environment, so spends much more of its time amongst the higher foliage than it does foraging at ground level. Coming from an isolated area which spills over from north western Queensland across the eastern border of Northern Territory, it gets its name from a mining area the parrakeets frequent which includes the towns of Cloncurry and Mount Isa; many bird watchers go there especially to see this distinctive sub-species.

In its tropical homeland it breeds between February and June. The courtship, nesting habits, incubation period, fledging age and general character of the Cloncurry are the same as the Barnard's Parrakeet, including the difficulty often encountered in re-mating adult aviary birds that have lost a partner of several seasons; but it does seem to be far more frequently bred and more often available nowadays in Britain than its larger relative.

EUCALYPTUS TREES in their many types provide a wide variety of sustenance in the form of nectar, pollen, blossom, seed and even insect life for the Cloncurry Parrakeet and its relatives - as well as affording shelter, nesting sites and camouflage against predators.

Colour Varieties

No colour varieties are known at present, but a **Blue** variety would be something to see - I hope no one attempts to introduce it via the Blue Barnard's, as this would lead to the ruination of both sub-species.

The PORT LINCOLN or BAUER'S PARRAKEET
Barnardius zonarius

Australia: Port Lincoln Parrot, Yellow-naped Parrot, or Yellow-banded Parrot.
France: Perruche à barbe bleue.
Germany: Bauer's Ringsittich.
Holland: Port Lincoln Parkiet.

Length: 14$^1/_2$in, 37cm.
Weight: cock 142-170gm, hen 121-136gm.

WITH BOLD PATTERNS of yellow on collar, lower breast and belly, glossy dark green on upper breast, wings and back, and black head with dark blue cheeks, the sturdy **Port Lincoln Parrakeet** *(Barnardius zonarius zonarius)* is unmistakeable. A red frontal band is present in some specimens, but missing or barely perceptible in others. Hens vary slightly in appearance by having a brownish cast to their heads, but difficulties occur in the sexing of this species, the usually larger heads and broader bills of cocks are sometimes almost matched in exceptional hens. The under-wing stripe is absent in adult cocks and usually missing in adult hens, immature cocks usually lack the wing stripe but it is said to be present in all immature hens.

Distribution and Habits in the Wild

Common in all its strongholds and particularly so in the wheat growing country of Western Australia, it is one of the most widely spread of the Australian parrots, reaching out from central Western Australia as far as southern areas of Northern Territory, and northern areas of South Australia - where it is represented by its doubtful sub-species *Barnardius zonarius myrtae*. The pale race - *Barnardius zonarius occidentalis* - is found in north-central Western Australia, apparently enclosed north of the curve of the Murchison River; it is lighter in coloration, greens are paler overall, and also the blue of the cheeks; the yellow plumage has a lemon tint, and the head is greyish.

Port Lincolns make themselves a success in virtually any type of habitat, whether forest, farm land or alongside water courses, but prefer open forest; in the most arid and inhospitable ranges of their distribution area they are nomadic, but this is due only to the necessity of their search for food and water. In these areas, the Port Lincoln relies on stunted growths of eucalyptus which are kept alive by underground streams, but in farming areas the species has been helped inadvertently by the provision of extra sources of water through the installation of artesian bore holes and pumps, and troughs for livestock.

These parrakeets are opportunist feeders and insects provide an important part of their diet; beside taking the available easily gathered wild produce of the locality, and raiding cereal crops and fruit orchards, they are also prepared to work for their living by excavating grubs from beneath the bark of trees, and by digging for bulbs like those of onion grass.

Like the Rosellas, Port Lincolns are usually seen in family groups, but gather in numbers where an abundance of food has been discovered. Tending to be a noisier species than Barnard's Parrakeet, their chatterings advertise their presence as they move across the feeding area. Their contact calls are pleasant whistles and steadily repeated double notes, with a more raucous rapidly repeated alarm call. Also - like the Rosellas - they are strong flyers, rising up to the perch from a low swooping flight path, with the final flourish of a spreading tail to break their speed.

Nesting in the Wild

Amid much chatter and with tails wagging from side to side, the parrakeets inspect their nests, and work on modifying the nest takes up a lot of the birds' time. Courtship and nesting habits are like the Barnard's, with hollow trunks or branches in the many species of eucalyptus being preferred as nest sites; up to seven eggs - but usually five - may be laid and they are often double brooded in the natural state. In the southern areas of their range they breed from August to February, but in the tropical areas of the Northern Territory the season runs from July to September.

From the commencement of the breeding cycle, the cock stands guard close by the nest hole, and it is necessary that he keeps the hen well supplied with regurgitated food, because she comes out of the nest rarely more than twice a day during incubation and for the first ten days of the hatchlings lives, feeding them on her own. After this time, as the young grow and become more demanding, both parents need to search for food and both go in and out of the nest to feed their young.

Aviculture in Britain

It is usual to leave nest-boxes in position the year round, because it is likely the birds will miss the season entirely if they are discouraged from nesting early. Port Lincolns are hardy and, with their strong bills, likely to be destructive to flimsy woodwork and thin wire if the fancy takes them - so their aviary should be built with this in mind.

Exceptionally cold springs can delay a regular breeding pair's efforts by up to two weeks, but it is usual for pairs to go to nest towards the latter part of March; those that are double brooded will have fledged their first clutch by mid May and have another clutch of eggs by the end of that month, with the second nest of young fledging at the end of July.

One breeder of recent years told me that his pair went to nest as late as April. Initially, a large nest-box measuring forty-four inches (940mm) high by eleven inches (280mm) square was used, but the first two seasons were disappointing as the hen laid and then broke her eggs. The following season a much smaller nest measuring twenty-eight inches (713mm) high by seven inches (178mm) square inside was used and success came. The box was hung under cover in a flight twelve feet long (3.65m), six feet wide (1.83m) and seven feet high (2.19m); four eggs were laid, incubation commenced from the second egg and took twenty-one days. Regular nest inspection was not possible because of the hen's aggressive disposition, however, three hatchlings were found to be in the nest towards the end of April and subsequently all four eggs hatched. They were reared well by their parents and fledged at six weeks old.

The birds' diet included parrakeet seed mixture, soaked seed, orange, apple, sweet corn (frozen from the previous year's crop), dandelion heads and a soft food mixture consisting of bread and milk with additions of vitamin/mineral powder, glucose, bone-meal and *'Vitalin'* dog food.

Provided that a resurgence in breeding Australian parrakeets can be maintained, and the work done by previous bird breeders is not wasted, the future of such handsome parrots as the Port Lincoln will be assured in European Aviaries.

Colour Varieties

Mutants have occurred - **Blues** - in which the yellow plumage of the wild type is replaced by white and green plumage by blue. Just a few years ago there was a Port Lincoln in a display cabinet with other parrots in the Natural History Museum in Kensington, it was a **Marine** specimen with cream replacing yellow and a dark glossy blue-green replacing the normal colour of the wings, upper breast and central tail feathers; most unusually, there was no label or notice to explain that the bird was not of the normal wild type coloration; at least one English breeder has bred this colour variety and is working to establish it.

The TWENTY-EIGHT or YELLOW-NAPED PARRAKEET
Barnardius zonarius semitorquatus

Australia: Twenty-eight Parrot, Yellow-naped Parrot, or Yellow-collared Parrot.
France: Perruche à Vingt-huit, or Perruche à collier jaune.
Germany: Kragensittich.
Holland: Twenty Eight Parkiet.

Length: 15$^{3}/_{4}$in, 40cm.
Weight: cock 142-191gm, hen 134-199gm.

FROM EAST TO WEST, the nominate race becomes variable; the size increases, the red frontal band becomes wider and more definite, and light green encroaches onto the belly until the integration with the **Twenty-eight Parrakeet** *(Barnardius zonarius semitorquatus)* is completed so that the lower abdomen of this sub-species is entirely light green. This last race is confined to the south-west corner of Western Australia and it is said to have been named after its three noted call which sounds like *'twen-ty-eight'* or *'chink-a-link'* - all races have clear ringing musical voices.

It is reported that numbers of Port Lincolns and Twenty-eights are caught in Western Australia and sent east for the bird trade, escapees have now established themselves in pockets adjacent to Melbourne, Sydney and Canberra. The fear is that they will spread, to the detriment of locally indigenous species of parrakeets because of their large size and aggressive nature, making it easy for them to commandeer nest sites and food supplies. Because of the free availability of these birds to the pet trade, they have not - so far - been a popular subject for serious parrakeet breeders in Australia.

Description
This is a very powerful and large parrakeet - bigger than the Port Lincoln - and some of the cock birds I have seen in England are outstanding for their enormous size. The two shades of green on the underparts is clearly delineated, dark laurel green on upper breast and lime green on the lower breast and belly.

Hens are slightly duller and often a lot smaller in the body and the head when compared with cocks, and have a narrower red frontal band as well as a slight brownish cast over the black of the head - most adult hens and all adult cocks do not show an underwing stripe.

Distribution and Habits in the Wild
The Twenty-eight nests in its native territory from August through to December, and is at home in dense forest, farm land and tree-lined streets of the suburban areas of towns - even in Perth itself. It is plentiful, as a direct result of the great increase in agricultural and fruit growing activities, and is regarded as an agricultural pest in Western Australia, especially by orchard keepers.

Away from the Twenty-eight's stronghold in the far south west corner of Western Australia, birds with yellow on the underparts begin to appear and continue to increase in number as they progress eastward, until populations of the pure Port Lincoln are finally reached in more central regions; it is believed that Twenty-eights were originally isolated from the nominate sub-species in ages past so that the two began to develop differing characteristics, and that the barriers which kept them apart became removed in the less distant past, so that their outriders finally met and bred and created intermediate forms.

Accommodation

As the largest of their genus, Twenty-eights look their best in a spacious aviary with at least a twenty feet long flight (6.09m); they will stay in reasonably good condition and go to nest in a flight fifteen feet long (4.56m), but the extra length helps prevent obesity, loss of condition and ultimate infertility. They can easily chew their way through nineteen gauge wire so their flight should be covered in at least sixteen gauge welded mesh - especially the roof, through which they have been frequently known to escape.

Woodwork comes in for unwelcome attention and needs to be protected with thin metal if bare areas of aviary framework are accessible to the birds; branches of non-toxic species - with leaves attached - should be provided regularly to satisfy their need to whittle and gnaw. The aggressive nature of these very large parrakeets, and their strength of bill, should be taken into account when choosing their adjacent neighbours; double wiring is recommended to prevent bills and toes being torn in skirmishes.

In the Aviary

Attempts at nesting can be expected from two years old, but success may not be achieved until they are in their third year at least. The courtship ritual is practically the same as that of Barnard's Parrakeet and the Rosellas with all the accompanying tail wagging, chattering, bowing and bobbing, strutting and wing shivering. Breeding commences from March to May, nesting attempts can be even earlier, but some breeders have found it best not to allow access to the nest-box too early in the year. Even so, this parrakeet is recognized as one of the hardiest, and is usually kept in aviaries with open fronted shelters throughout England and Wales - Scotland might be a different matter.

It has been found advisable by some breeders to provide a natural nest log if possible, and also to always set the nest at a slight angle to prevent the hen dropping straight down onto her eggs and breaking them. The clutch of eggs is slightly smaller on average for this larger sub-species, usually four sometimes five, and the duller immature birds acquire their adult brilliance at between a year and eighteen months old.

Twenty-eights are well established in British aviculture and should remain so, as long as hybridization with the Port Lincoln and partly yellow-bellied hybrids does not persist; specimens are quite often advertised for sale, but whether these are all pure Twenty-eights is a matter for the purchaser to judge.

Colour Varieties

Rare colour varieties of the Twenty-eight are being established, including a golden yellow **Lutino** with an orange-red frontal band, as well as a true **Blue** mutant of especially deep and lustrous shades.

In nineteen ninety-four Mr F. White - a parrakeet breeder of many years experience - sent me feather samples off a Twenty-eight cock in which the underlying yellow ground colour was changing to red; the result of this **Red Suffusion** was the alteration of the normal dark laurel green areas to deep bronze, with an orange cast given to the paler lime green plumage. Unfortunately, this type of colour change is nowadays usually regarded as detrimental and - as far as is known - does not indicate a definite inheritable variety; suggestions as to its cause include symptoms relating to the possible presence of blood parasites (which can be passed to offspring), as well as the possibility of long term liver and/or kidney damage, or a dietary deficiency due to an inability to fully assimilate nutrients. Of course, there is also the possibility that parrakeets of this genus will finally develop a mutation which brings about an inheritable spread of red ground colour - as with the Ruby Eastern Rosella.

THE PILEATED'S UNUSUAL BILL has evolved as a specialized tool which helps it to reach 'hard-to-get-at' seeds such as those of casuarina *(below, right)* and hakea, but most importantly the cup shaped seed capsules of the marri *(Eucalyptus calophylla)*, which provide their main source of food and with which they are strongly associated; the largest and oldest trees maintain a continuous supply of seeds at various stages of ripening. An increase in the felling of mature trees could well have a detrimental effect on the birds' future survival. The unripe seed capsule is easily opened, but when fully ripe is extremely hard, it is then that the Pileated makes good use of its specialized bill; with deft movements, the seeds are extracted with the upper mandible inserted down the narrow neck of the 'gum nut' as this is twisted around with the foot - leaving only slight indentations on its outer lip. Many other seeds, berries and fruit beside marri are eaten, as well as insects and their larvae. Other Australian parrots beside the Pileated seek out infestations of an insect pest which attaches itself to the undersides of leaves, and - presumably - are plant parasites. These soft bodied 'psyllid lerps' *(Psyllidae)* protect themselves by building up a hard scaly shell over their exposed uppersides, and it is this exuded carbohydrate covering that attracts the parrots - they enjoy both sugar coating and the soft-bodied insect it shields. Pileateds are so dextrous that they can scrape or lever the insects off without removing leaves from the branches.

In the aviary, though eager for extra fruit and greenfood, Pileateds will otherwise thrive on the same diet that suits Rosellas. Breeders find that Pileateds especially enjoy apple, any type of greenstuff, pyracantha and hawthorn berries, unripe seeding grass and even thistle heads. A regular supply of twigs and branches is needed to try to divert attention from wooden aviary framework. Soft food mixtures such as *'Ce-de', 'Milupa'* baby food, bread and milk and cake are appreciated - grated carrot can be added. Insectivorous mixtures are sometimes given, and mealworms could be a good clean type of livefood to offer.

Keith Gallagher - from New South Wales - has kept Pileateds for seventeen years; the diet he gives his birds is extensive, but only a few of these items would be impossible to find in Britain. His diet includes: small seeds plus, sunflower, peanuts in shell, sprouted sunflower, sprouted oats, apples, oranges, mandarins, pears, banana, grapes, passion fruit, kiwi fruit, watermelon, rock melon, paddy melon, pineapple, corn-on-the-cob, boiled maize, endive, silver beet, celery, parsley, chickweed, capsicum, beetroot, cotoneaster and hawthorn berries, seeding grasses, 'gum nuts', wattle flower and native tree branches for whittling.

A 'true' pair was housed in a mixed collection and - in October of the year - produced two infertile clutches; the bird believed to be a cock was in fact a hen, which illustrates that even experienced Australian breeders can have difficulty in sexing this species. The two hens were kept in a large communal aviary which measured twenty-two feet (6.7m) wide by forty seven feet (14.3m) long and also housed nine pairs of Cockatiels, seven pairs of Red-rumped Parrakeets, as well as Bourke's, Barraband's, Kings, Princess of Wales, Diamond Doves and Quail! Partners were found for the two hens and both laid - one six eggs and one five eggs - and hatched out full clutches; the eleven young were removed for hand-rearing at around two weeks old to make them steadier. Natural log nests were used, measuring nineteen and a half inches (495mm) high and eleven and three-quarter inches (298mm) wide, with an entrance hole four inches (101mm) in diameter.

The next year they were later going to nest; a larger selection of logs was given and the hens - spoilt for choice - took a long time to decide which to use! One chosen nest had to be moved because a cock Barnard's in an adjacent flight began feeding the hen. Nine young were hatched by the two hens, but this time only two survived. In both seasons the hens gave the impression that they would produce second clutches, but failed to do so, and neither hen used the same nest twice. These unusual results fly in the face of all warnings against including adult pairs of broad-tails in mixed collections; but - on this occasion - it is safer to regard Mr Gallagher's experience as an exception that proves the rule, and not attempt to reproduce his method.

3. The Single Species of Genus Purpureicephalus

The PILEATED or RED-CAPPED PARRAKEET
Purpureicephalus spurius

Australia: Pileated Parrot, Red-capped Parrot, Western King Parrot, or Hookbill.
France: Perruche à tête pourpre.
Germany: Rotkappensittich.
Holland: Roodkap Parkiet.

Length: $14^1/_2$in, 37cm.
Weight: cock 105-156gm, hen 98-135gm.

UNIQUE AMONG the Australian parrots for its appearance, behaviour and calls, the **Pileated Parrakeet** *(Purpureicephalus spurius)* is one of the most unusual and attractive of the broad-tails. Similarities in appearance with the Rosellas include the contrasting cheek patches, red under-tail coverts and typical blue and green 'broad-tail'; pugnacious Rosella and *Barnardius* species should not be housed next to this parrakeet, fighting between jealous cocks will occur. The Pileated has long been prized among European bird breeders; but it is not always as freely available in Britain as on the continent. The first breeding in Britain took place in nineteen hundred and nine, and in Australia at Adelaide Zoo in nineteen thirty-eight. Breeders refer to its shy and secretive habits and the nervousness of its young during the fledgling stage. These characteristics are exasperating to bird keepers wanting to admire their Pileateds instead of just catching fleeting glimpses as they dive into their shelter.

The Pileated's closest relatives are now believed to be the Rosella-Barnard's group; past suggestions that it should be regarded as a close relative of the Horned Parrakeets have been rejected, but similarities in habits with this genus, which is closely related to the Kakarikis, need examining. Young of Horned Parrakeets *(Eunymphicus)* and Kakarikis *(Cyanoramphus)* have distinct white spots on the backs of their heads which appear once the secondary grey down has grown through; nestling Pileateds also show this feature once the thin white hatchling down has been replaced by grey. The species - believed to be the most primitive of the broad-tails - has been afforded a genus of its own, and is said to be the only survivor of an ancient group of closely related psittacines that became extinct less than a million years ago. These extinct parrots lived at a time when the now parched interior of Australia was covered with forest; it is believed that they were the forebears of the existing more recently evolved broad-tailed parrakeets. There is mention of a dubious sub-species which has darker greens and violet-blues - *Purpureicephalus spurius carteri* - recorded in the Broome Hill area.

Description
The plumage of the cock is vivid; the cap is red (so giving its other name of Red-capped Parrakeet), large lime green patches cover the sides of the face, the green wings have blackish flights with outer edges of blue; the lime green rump acts as a strong visual contact signal when the birds are in flight; green central tail feathers have dark blue tips, and the pale blue lateral tail feathers have whitish tips. Under-tail coverts and thighs are red, and the breast and belly are a rich violet-mauve. The eyes are dark; the greyish bill is narrow and elongated, and the lower mandible holds the upper continually open, leaving a noticeable gap; protruding bristle like feathers fan out from the corners of the mouth, it has been surmised that these may protect the exposed tongue or help in collecting pollen which is then licked away. Hen Pileateds are duller than their partners - though variable in this respect - with a grey tinge to the mauve-blue of their breasts and bellies when compared with those of cocks. Their caps are sometimes scattered with green, and even the brightest hens have a line of green feathers

immediately above the eye, which cocks lack. Yellow-green edging is present on the hens' under-tail coverts, giving a barred effect, but this lessens with age. Their heads and bills are smaller and finer, and the under-wing stripe - lacking in cocks - is present. Though difficult to sex in immature plumage, some breeders find young uncoloured hens have more white spotting on the under-wing than cocks, also there is more yellow-green edging to the under-tail coverts. Experienced breeders sex their youngsters by comparing heads and bills, with cocks' heads being larger than those of hens, and hens' bills being smaller and narrower.

Fledgling Pileateds differ greatly in appearance from their parents; they are much smaller, take a long time growing to their full size and are devoid of brilliant colour. Their upper parts are dull green, their underparts are greyish brown with a bluer wash on the belly, face patches lack vivid colour, under-tail coverts are pale red and there is only a narrow rusty red frontal band instead of a red cap. Young cocks begin to show red patches in the cap area at five months, but acquisition of full adult colour takes from fifteen months to as long as two years - even so, year old birds have been known to breed.

Distribution, Habits in the Wild and Nesting

Pileateds are a familiar sight to residents and visitors in Perth, and are known to breed in park land near the city centre. In their wild places - at the present time - they are still common in their strongholds of the south-western corner of Western Australia, gradually thinning in numbers at the inland edges of their range. They live in dense forests and woodlands bordering farmland, frequenting parks and orchards where they are such pests that apple and pear growers are allowed open seasons to kill them off. Young birds especially - in company with a scattering of adults - band together in large numbers and attack the growing fruit; in doing so noisy youngsters make themselves conspicuous targets, but older birds tend to be more wary, remain hidden and feed silently, with only falling discarded food giving them away. When disturbed, adults take to a topmost lookout branch, stretch up in an erect stance and issue loud alarm calls, which sound like *'krrrick, krrrick'*. As a means of staying in contact with their companions, characteristic harsh metallic calls are given as they fly, and, though their flight lacks the characteristic swooping of the Rosellas, its action is swift and silent, alternating between rapid beating of the wings and gliding; the flaring of the tail on alighting is neither as marked nor as flourishing as that of Rosellas.

During courtship, the strutting cock Pileated drops his wings to display the elevated feathers of his rump, fans and holds his tail high, and raises his red cap feathers until they resemble a crest; his routine closely resembles that of the Hooded Parrakeet (of the genus *Psephotus*) but the Pileated also makes harsh, chattering calls to his mate. The threat display to interlopers and rivals consists of raucous chattering, raised head feathers, open bill, jutting shoulders and flaring tail; hens can show more spite than cocks. Hand-reared cocks make these threatening actions as a direct warning to their owners in defence of their hens and nests. An Australian breeder found that a cock would breed with two hens in the same flight, the more dominant hen being the first to go down; two trios bred successfully for at least three seasons.

In the wild - being in the southern hemisphere - nesting commences as early as August and carries on through to December, with pairs preferring marri trees for the nest hollow which is generally situated at some height. In Britain, cocks have been seen feeding their hens as early as January, but hens usually come into lay in this country between May and June, with some breeders finding them as late as July and August. In the aviary - like the other large broad-tails - cock Pileateds have to be watched for aggressive tendencies towards their hens and young. Even so, cocks are not always the dominant partner with this species, one British breeder found his hen to be master until disadvantaged by becoming cumbersome as she filled with eggs; once she was heavy and less agile the cock would turn and take his revenge by giving her a severe beating. If flight feathers were removed from one wing - so as to slow him down - he immediately went into a sulk and totally ignored his partner, even though she called to him for attention; in this way the season was wasted.

Known for their nervous disposition when first beginning to incubate their eggs, hen Pileateds will sit more tightly as they become broodier. I remember visiting the aviaries of the late W. Partridge in Worcestershire during one spring in the early 'sixties, and being shown around the innumerable aviaries. The block of flights housing nesting pairs of Pileateds was not even approached for fear the slightest disturbance would cause desertion. Obviously, seclusion is most important and interference will cause nervous hens to desert; also, the owner's interference has caused cocks to become belligerent towards their hens. In Britain, single broods are usual, but if the first clutch is infertile the hen will commence laying a second clutch about two weeks later. As with most Australian Parrakeets, a dry warm spring can cause them to miss the season and go into a moult as early as the beginning of June.

Taking into account the wide variety of sizes of logs and boxes they are reported to have used, Pileateds do not seem fussy about the type of nest offered; the clutch of eggs may range from three to seven - more in rare cases - and quite large nests of young can be reared. Bathing is enjoyed, and saturated hens have been seen returning to their eggs or hatchlings with no apparent harm caused. Incubation takes nineteen to twenty days; the hen feeds the young for the first couple of weeks from regurgitated food passed to her by the cock; both partners then begin to share the work of feeding the young. The young fledge at around five weeks when great care must be taken to see that they do not damage themselves through taking fright; leafy branches placed at the ends of the flight prevent collision with the wire.

Pileateds show a greater interest in whittling than Rosellas and can cause extensive damage to unprotected woodwork in an aviary. This destructive tendency can be dangerous and birds have died after ingested splinters have pierced the gut. One breeder found that his hen Pileated continually gnawed its nest-box until its eggs rolled out of the holes onto the floor; it continued to gnaw away the inside of the repaired box until the lid fell part way into the nest chamber. Tomato boxes used as temporary nest lids were destroyed at the rate of one a week! These parrakeets can also use their narrow but strong bills to gnaw their way out through thin wire mesh, so only strong mesh should be used to cover the flight.

In Australia

Pileateds can be legally trapped and sold in Western Australia, and a great many have been sent to bird keepers in the east of the country, but Australian breeders are wary of purchasing recently caught birds which are exceptionally nervous, and likely to damage themselves in confinement as well as unsettle the established aviary stock; in this way a breeding season can be ruined. With wild caught birds, the aviary is covered with leafy branches, with further arrangements of thick foliage being set up inside the aviary, so giving them cover in which to hide and preventing them from being flushed into a mad dashing flight. Once the birds have become used to their surroundings and have settled down, the foliage can be gradually removed - but this may take a long time. Novices are advised to obtain only aviary bred stock; hand-reared Pileateds completely lack these wild and nervous traits.

Colour Varieties

Pied, Cinnamon and **Dilute** examples are known in Australia. A Worcestershire breeder produced a Pied youngster which moulted out with yellow patches amongst the green, and white patches on the breast. As far as is known no **Blues** or **Lutinos** yet exist; my projections show the expected results - it is probable that the Lutino will have a slight pink cast to the white of the breast and belly. In the wild, some members of an isolated flock showed a red stripe across their rumps; and there are reports of wild cock birds being seen with maroon patches or bars across the shoulders.

AUSTRALIA:

Features and Areas relevant to the Text and Distribution of the Species and Sub-species

4. *The Colour Plates & Distribution Maps*

IN THE MAPS which accompany the set of colour plates, the distribution areas of each of the groups - the 'White-cheeked' Rosellas of *Platycercus*, the 'Blue-cheeked' Rosellas of *Platycercus*, and the members of *Barnardius* - are outlined in a way which shows the home range of each species and sub-species in comparison with that of its closest relatives. The single member of *Purpureicephalus* is shown on a separate section below the map for *Barnardius*. The map which overlays the approximate distribution areas of the three genera illustrates the few ranges in which members of *Platycercus* share territory with members of *Barnardius*, and the one area - in Western Australia - where all three genera are represented.

Approximate Distribution Areas

The distribution areas have been arrived at through studying the most prominent literature on the subject. The recorded distribution areas have apparently been established through plotting the most outlying positions of many sightings resulting from observations made by numerous individuals, throughout a mass of localities over many years. Therefore, unless bordered by impenetrable natural physical obstacles, the boundaries of these distribution areas can only be regarded as approximate, and where vast areas are concerned the variability of estimations must be greatly magnified. Obviously, the parrakeets do not populate an area evenly throughout its entire expanse; the named species or sub-species may even be extremely common in some localities within a given area, and sparse or even non-existent in others. In addition, some populations are known to be sedentary by nature, through clinging to a particular type of habitat which provides their basic needs of water, food and nesting sites, while others may wander great distances in following the transitory flowering, fruiting and seeding of various food plants and trees - of both natural and cultivated sources. This can cause fluctuations throughout the year and even over a cycle of years; as can flood, drought and natural occurrences such as bush fires, which can also bring about displacements or the destruction of whole sections of wild populations on a large scale.

Colour Varieties

Some of the varieties shown in the following illustrations are well established, some are extremely rare, a few have yet to come into existence and are a glimpse into the future of this branch of aviculture, and others result through combining one variety with another. As well as the breeding patterns for many single colour varieties, programmes spread over several breeding seasons for producing combination and compound colour varieties, in many species of psittacine birds, are contained within ***The Manual of Colour Breeding***; this manual can be used in the production of established colour varieties of the parrakeets illustrated in *this* book. For example, in programmes for the **Eastern Rosella**, clear instructions are given for breeding: **Cinnamon Dilute** (page **102**), **Cinnamon Lutino** (*Sex-linked* page **115**, *Recessive* page **116**), **Cinnamon Melanistic** (page **118**), **Cinnamon Ruby** (page **121**), **Dilute Ruby** (page **128**), **Dominant Pied Ruby** (page **165**), **Rubino** (*Sex-linked* page **93**, *Recessive* page **96**) and even **Dominant Pied Melanistic** (page **164**). The effect on pigment and patterns of inheritance for **Albino, Lutino, Cinnamon, Dilute, Fallow, the Dark Factor, Grey, Pied, Blue, Marine, Violet, Ruby,** etc, are among the topics which are thoroughly examined.

The Colour Plates

The illustrations of parrakeets in this book are especially designed to allow for comparisons to be easily made between species, sub-species and colour varieties, regarding: differences in plumage pattern, physical characteristics and size - from the smallest, the Stanley Rosella, to the largest, the Twenty-eight Parrakeet.

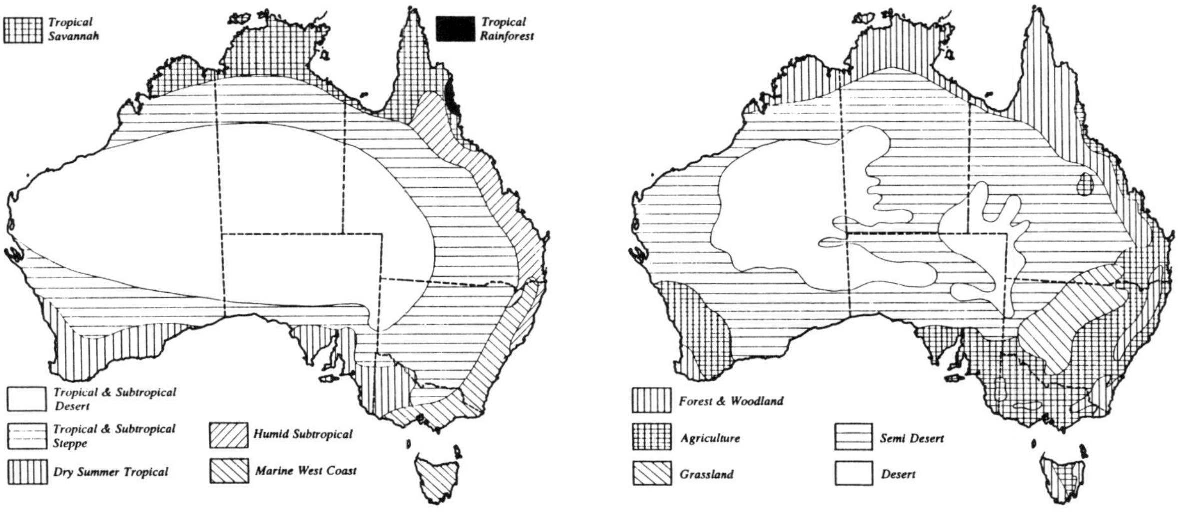

THE GIVEN AREAS of climate and land cover can only be regarded as generalisations, and the following should be taken into account: vast areas of northern Australia have been used for cattle rearing, while even greater combined areas of south west and eastern Australia are sheep rearing country by long tradition; the present rate of spread of agricultural is unknown, while the clearing of forest and timber production on one hand, and tree planting and conservation work on the other, means that great areas must be in a continually changing state - and all this without considering the variables resulting from a growing and changing human population, increasing industry - and long term climatic cycles.

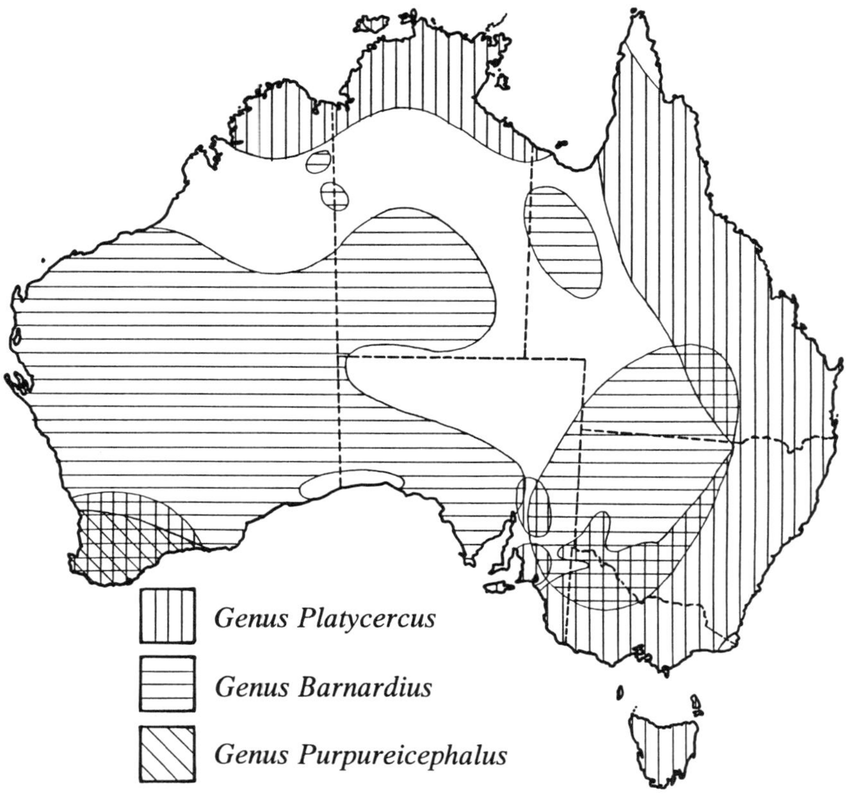

AUSTRALIA: Climate (top left) and Land Cover (top right) in relation to the Distribution of the Three Genera (bottom)

Plate 1: Eastern, Mealy, Brown's and Stanley Rosellas

Identification and Distribution in the Wild of Examples on Plate 1

The 'White-cheeked' Group:

1. Pale-headed Rosella *Platycercus adscitus palliceps.*
2. Blue-cheeked Rosella *Platycercus adscitus adscitus.*
3. Mealy or Blue Rosella; transitional form laying between the Pale-headed and the Blue-cheeked, showing golden yellow edging to mantle feathers and violet blue abdomen; cock **3a**, hen **3b**.
4. Natural hybrid; Pale-headed Rosella x Golden-mantled Eastern Rosella; examples are found where the distribution areas of the two overlap.
5. Golden-mantled Eastern Rosella *Platycercus eximius cecilae.*
6. Eastern or Red Rosella *Platycercus eximius eximius;* cock **6a**, hen **6b**.
7. Tasmanian Eastern Rosella *Platycercus eximius diemenensis.*
8. 'Green-backed' Stanley Rosella *Platycercus icterotis icterotis;* cock **8a**, hen **8b**.
9. 'Red-backed' Stanley Rosella *Platycercus icterotis xanthogenys;* cock **9a**, hen **9b**.
10. Blue-cheeked Northern or Kimberley Northern Rosella *Platycercus venustus hilli.*
11. Brown's or Northern Rosella *Platycercus venustus venustus.*

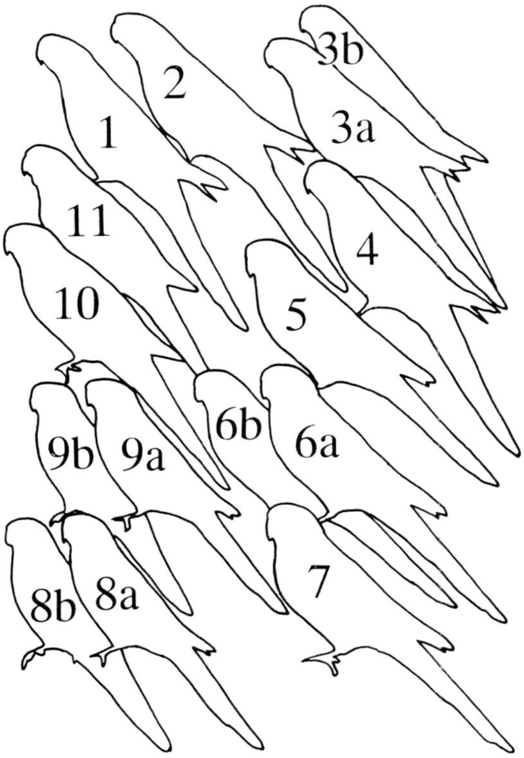

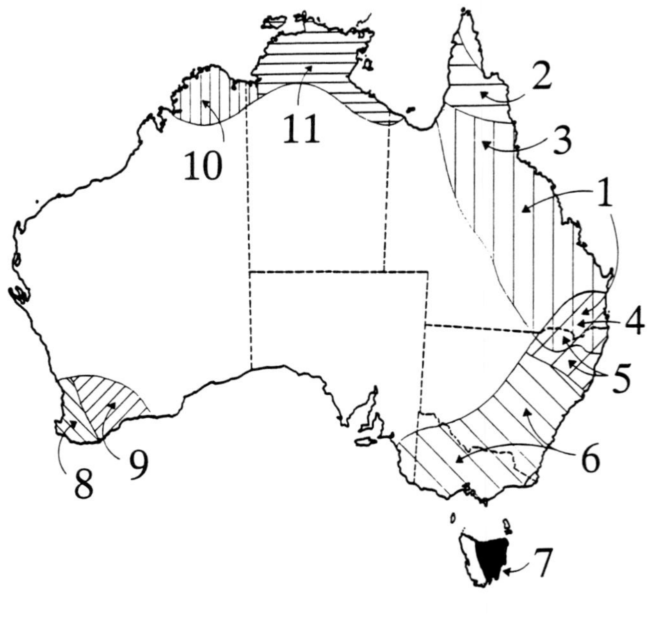

Identification of Examples on Plate 2

Colour Varieties of the Eastern Rosella;

1. Melanistic or Black; cock **1a**, hen **1b**.
2. Cinnamon Melanistic (combination of Cinnamon and Melanistic)*.
3. Ruby; type with pinkish tail and yellow markings on mantle and wings **3a**, type with green-blue tail and green markings on mantle and wings **3b**.
4. Dominant Pied Ruby (combination of Dominant Pied and Ruby, showing most desirable form with mostly white wings and tail).
5. Cinnamon Ruby (combination of Cinnamon and Ruby).
6. Dilute Ruby (combination of Dilute and Ruby).
7. Lutino.
8. Rubino (combination of Ruby and Ino).
9. Creamino (combination of Ino and Marine)*.
10. Marine*.
11. Blue.
12. Dominant Pied Normal; heavily variegated example **12a**, almost completely variegated example **12b**.
13. Dilute Normal; examples vary, darker type **13a**, paler type **13b**.
14. Cinnamon Normal (Australian variety with chocolate wing patches).
15. Cinnamon Normal (European variety, with fawn wing patches; sometimes described as Isabel).

Those varieties marked with an asterisk* are not known to exist at present but are the artist's projections of future developments which would be of most interest and are likely to occur.

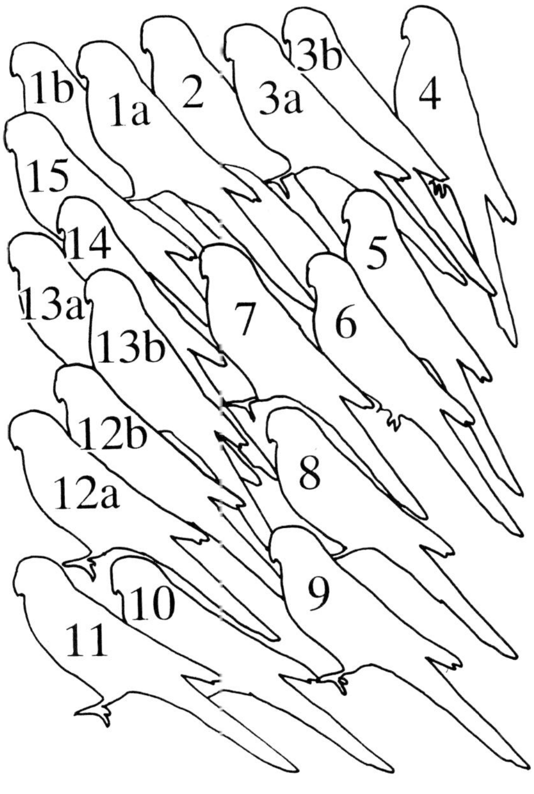

Plate 2: Colour Varieties of Eastern Rosella

Plate 3: Colour Varieties of Mealy, Brown's and Stanley Rosellas

Identification of Examples on Plate 3

Colour aberrations and varieties of Mealy, Brown's and Stanley Rosellas:

1. Pied Mealy Rosella.
2. Lutino Mealy Rosella*.
3. Blue Mealy Rosella*.
4. Red-flecked Brown's (often a good indication of hybrid blood, though some pure bred specimens are said to show the fault - it is *not* a colour variety).
5. Cinnamon Brown's Rosella*.
6. Blue Brown's Rosella*.
7. Blue Stanley Rosella; cock **7a**, hen **7b**.
8. Lutino Stanley Rosella; cock **8a**, hen **8b**.

Those marked with an asterisk* are not known to exist at present but are the artist's projections of future developments which would be of most interest and are likely to occur.

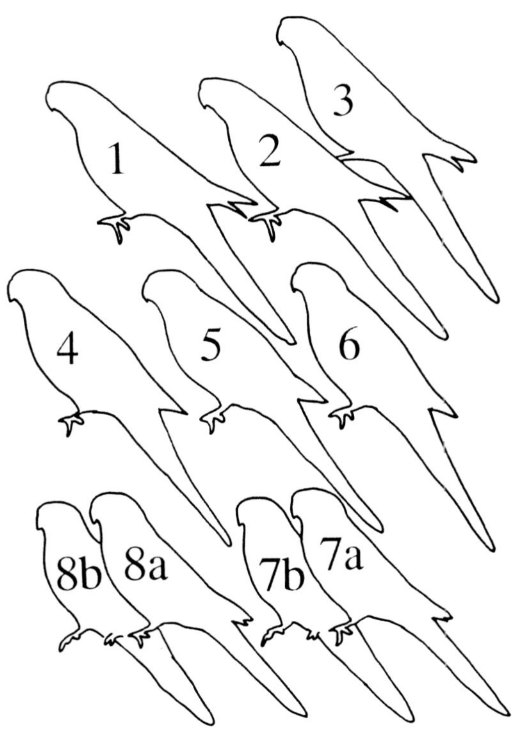

Identification and Distribution in the Wild of Examples on Plate 4

The 'Blue-cheeked' group:

1. Pennant's or Crimson Rosella *Platycercus elegans elegans;* cock **1a**, hen **1b**.
2. Northern Pennant's Rosella *Platycercus elegans nigrescens.*
3. Kangaroo Island Pennant's Rosella *Platycercus elegans melanoptera.*
4. Yellow or Yellow-rumped Rosella *Platycercus flaveolus;* pure bred and most desirable type, with hens as yellow as cocks.
5. Yellow Rosella *Platycercus flaveolus;* red-orange suffusion can show hybrid blood though some pure bred specimens are highly coloured.
6. Yellow Rosella of hybrid blood; a type which has been derived from Yellow Rosella x Adelaide, showing in an undesirable 'brassy' buff colour throughout, with orange suffusion.
7. Adelaide Rosella *Platycercus adelaidae adelaidae;* dark orange southern type.
8. Adelaide Rosella *Platycercus adelaidae subadelaidae;* paler northern type.
9. Tasmanian Rosella *Platycercus caledonicus;* type showing lemon ground colour and lacking extensive orange suffusion; original reference, Dr H.D. Groen, Holland.
10. Tasmanian Rosella *Platycercus caledonicus;* type showing extensive orange suffusion.

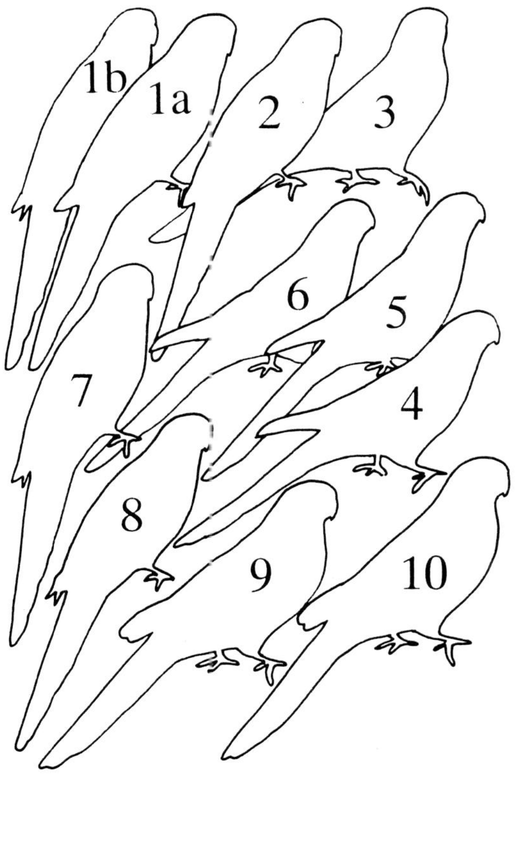

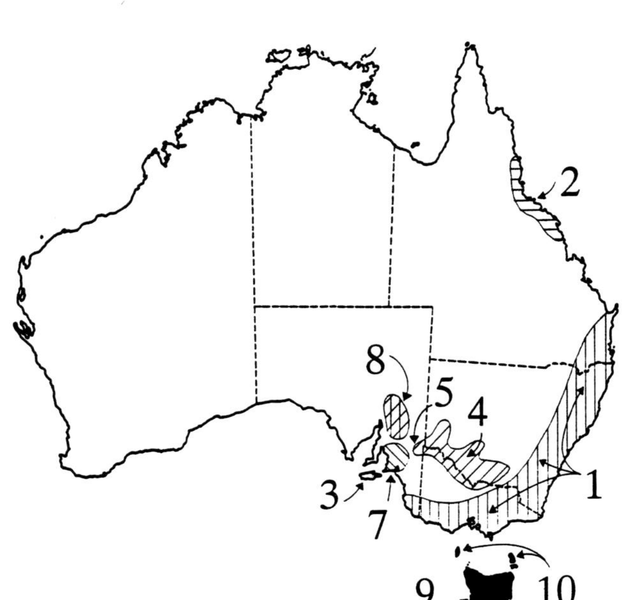

Plate 4: Pennant's, Adelaide, Yellow & Tasmanian Rosellas

Plate 5: Colour Varieties of Pennant's Rosella

Identification of Examples on Plate 5

Colour varieties of Pennant's Rosella:

1. Albino*.
2. Cinnamon Blue.
3. Blue; type with heavy melanin suffusion.
4. Blue; type with very little melanin suffusion.
5. Dilute Normal; 'Red, White and Blue' type; variety from back **5a**, variety from front **5b**.
6. Dilute Blue; 'White and Blue' type, a combination of Dilute Normal (**5**) and Blue (**3**).
7. Rubino*; the Ino form of the Pennant.
8. Cinnamon Normal.
9. Blue-bellied Normal.

Those marked with an asterisk* are not known to exist at present but are the artist's projections of future developments which would be of most interest and are likely to occur.

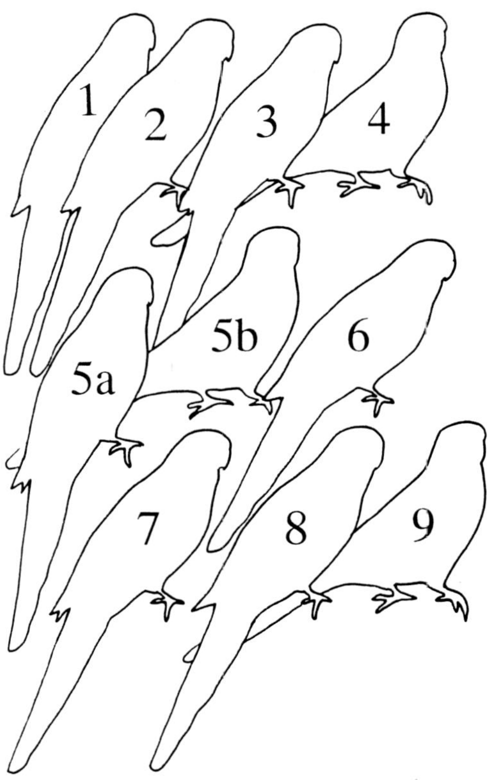

Identification of Examples on Plate 6

Colour varieties of Yellow, Pennant's and Adelaide Rosellas:

1. Lutino Yellow Rosella*.
2. Dilute Yellow Rosella.
3. Blue Yellow Rosella*.
4. 'Yellow' (Dilute) Pennant' Rosella; comparison should be made with the projection of a Dilute Adelaide Rosella (**8**).
5. Dilute Blue Pennant's Rosella; combination of 'Yellow' Pennant's Rosella (**4**) with Blue Pennant's Rosella (**Plate 5:** example number **3**).
6. Cinnamon Adelaide Rosella.
7. Lutino Adelaide Rosella.
8. Dilute Adelaide Rosella*.

Those marked with an asterisk* are not known to exist at present but are the artist's projections of future developments which could possibly occur.

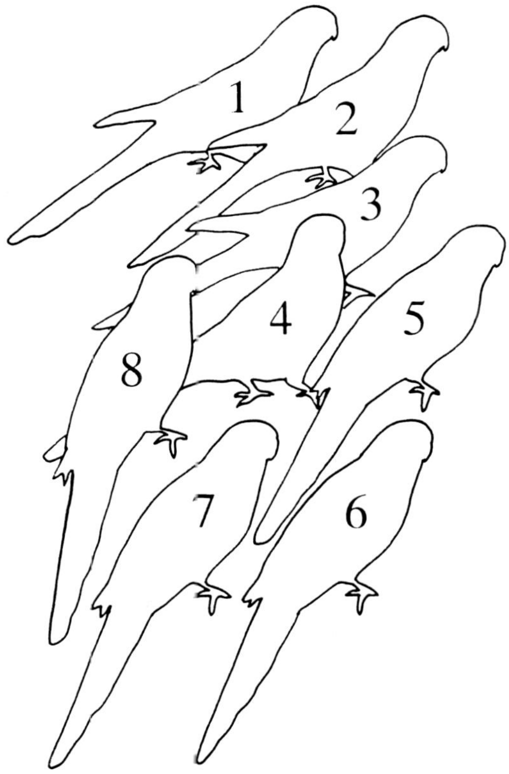

Plate 6: Colour Varieties of Yellow, Pennant's and Adelaide Rosellas

Plate 7: The Genus Barnardius & the Pileated Parrakeet

Identification and Distribution in the Wild of Examples on Plate 7

The Genus *Barnardius* and the Pileated Parrakeet:

1. Port Lincoln Parrakeet *Barnardius zonarius zonarius.*
2. Port Lincoln Parrakeet *Barnardius zonarius occidentalis;* pale western sub-species.
3. Examples of transitional types between the Port Lincoln and Twenty-eight Parrakeets; type closest to the Port Lincoln **3a**, type closest to the Twenty-eight **3b**.
4. Twenty-eight Parrakeet *Barnardius zonarius semitorquatus,* cock **4a**, hen **4b**.
5. Natural hybrid; Port Lincoln Parrakeet x Barnard's Parrakeet; their appearance is variable and examples are found where the distribution areas of the two species are closest, in south and central areas of Flinders Ranges, South Australia.
6. Barnard's Parrakeet *Barnardius barnardi barnardi,* cock **6a**, hen **6b.**
7. Barnard's Parrakeet *Barnardius barnardi whitei;* smaller sub-species in which cocks have dark green backs; found in western fringe of the species' range.
8. Cloncurry Parrakeet *Barnardius barnardi macgillivrayi,* cock **8a**, hen **8b**.
9. Pileated or Red-capped Parrakeet *Purpureicephalus spurius;* cock **9a**, hen **9b**.

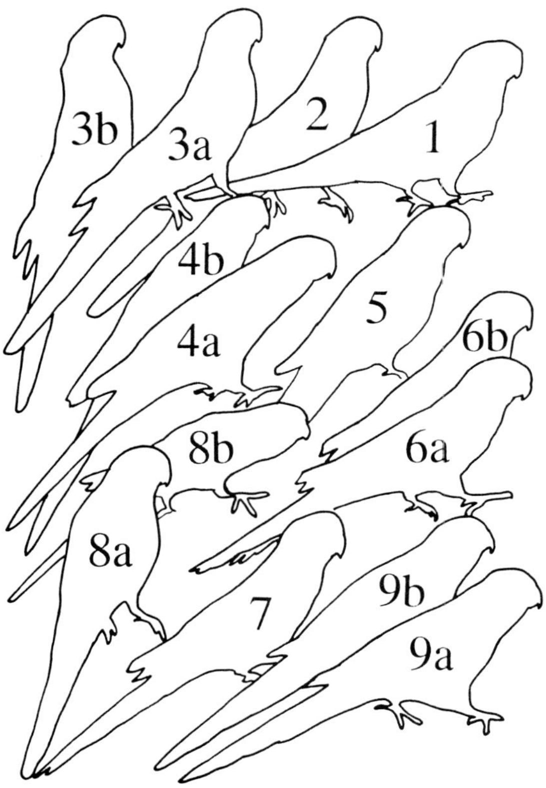

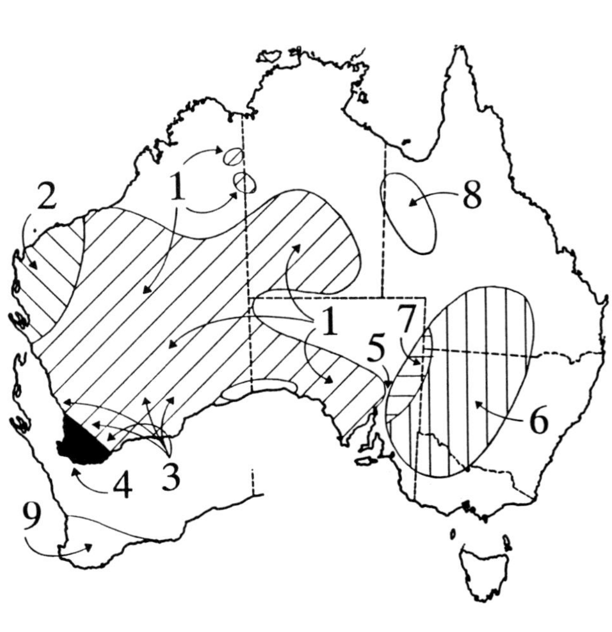

Identification of Examples on Plate 8

Colour Varieties of Twenty-eight, Port Lincoln, Barnard's, Cloncurry and Pileated Parrakeets:

1. Lutino Twenty-eight Parrakeet.
2. Blue Twenty-eight Parrakeet.
3. Dilute Twenty-eight Parrakeet.
4. Blue Port Lincoln Parrakeet.
5. Marine Port Lincoln Parrakeet.
6. Lutino Barnard's Parrakeet*.
7. Blue Barnard's Parrakeet.
8. Pied Normal Barnard's Parrakeet.
9. Blue Cloncurry Parrakeet*.
10. Lutino Pileated Parrakeet*.
11. Dilute Normal Pileated Parrakeet.
12. Pied Normal Pileated Parrakeet.
13. Cinnamon Normal Pileated Parrakeet*.
14. Blue Pileated Parrakeet*.

Those marked with an asterisk* are not known to exist at present but are the artist's projections of future developments which would be of most interest and are likely to occur.

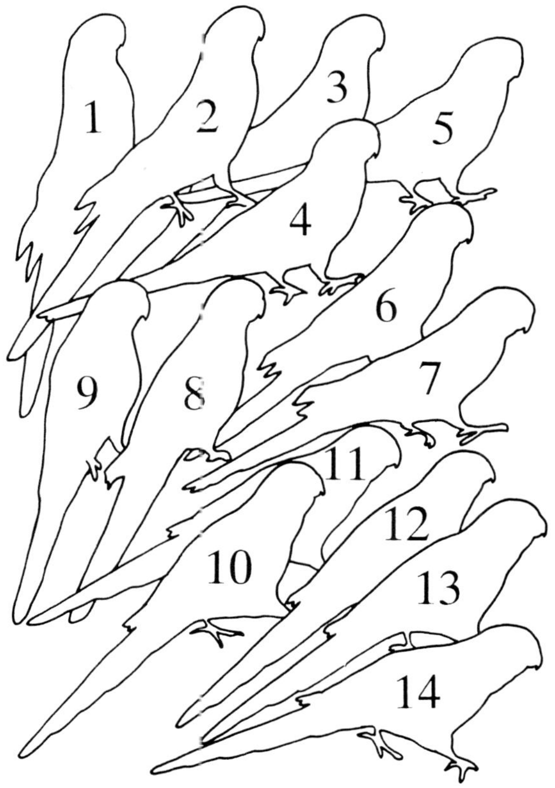

Plate 8: Colour Varieties of Genus Barnardius & The Pileated Parrakeet

5. *The Rosella Character*

THE WHOLE OF THE ROSELLA GROUP share certain desirable qualities as far as the aviculturist is concerned; their good looks and lively characters are obvious assets, and - though not over productive - they are relatively easily bred when compared with other psittacines. British breeders consider them to be hardy, they can survive our winters without heat and - unlike some Asiatic parrakeets - they are not prone to frost-bitten toes. I have seen long escaped Golden-mantled Rosellas feeding happily on winter gleanings from fields and hedgerows, the scarlet and gold of their plumage glowing brightly against the snow spattered English landscape.

Because of their full wide feathered tails they are known as 'broad-tails' and belong to a group - the tribe *Platycercini* - which also includes the Pileated Parrakeet, the members of *Barnardius* (e.g. the Port Lincoln) and *Psephotus* (e.g. the Redrump), the *Neophema* Grass Parrakeets, the Budgerigar, the Kakariki-Horned-Shining Parrot group, the Ground Parrot and Night Parrot, and even the Swift Parrakeet. In addition, all of these have - in comparison with each individual's size - stout thick set bills which lack red or pink, and set them aside from the 'coral-billed' parrots which include Kings, Crimson-wings, members of *Polytelis* (e.g. Barraband's Parrakeet), the Asiatic Parrakeets and Eclectus Parrots.

All the Rosella species display certain shared visual features: the large contrasting cheek patches, the black wing patch with its surrounding shades of blue, tails with dark green-blue central feathers and paler blue lateral feathers - and mantle and back feathers with blackish centres and coloured margins. When Rosellas take off in fright, giving vent to their characteristic strident alarm calls, these visual features act as additional strong warning signals to the accompanying birds, but, when the parrakeets are feeding on the ground or amongst foliage, the broken colours act as effective camouflage and help them to remain hidden from enemies.

Behaviour

The courtship and threat displays of the Rosellas are further shared mannerisms; they fan and vigorously shake their tails from side to side, make bowing movements and carefully touch the perch with their bill or cere as they do so; at the same time, elevating the feathers of their head, cheeks and breast to make themselves look larger and more impressive; as if perplexed, with rapid movements, a Rosella will scratch its head with its foot from over the back of its wing. In the absence of receptive hens, cocks in breeding condition will make violent jerking movements of the head and produce regurgitated food, daubing it on twigs and perches.

Apart from the occasional sharp screams of alarm calls, the Rosellas have pleasant chatterings and musical notes most commonly repeated in a staccato fashion; a call which sounds like *'cock-eee'* is typical, as well as quieter calls which sound like *'chink-a-link'*. The larger species have deeper, slightly louder voices than the smaller species. If neighbours are reasonable, it is unlikely that these parrakeets will cause complaints about noise.

Temperament

Pugnacious behaviour is another trait which is common to the whole genus, even though this can be measured from a lesser to a greater extent between the species. In my experience, the most violent is the Mealy, who also delights in acting as a scaremonger to the rest of the inhabitants of an aviary block by giving needless alarm calls; the Mealy cock dashes about the flight sending all the other parrakeets close by into a mad panic.

The least troublesome in this respect is the little cock Stanley, but even he can be murderous in particular situations. From this it will be clear that it is unwise to house Rosella species in adjoining flights, otherwise an entire breeding season may be wasted by fighting and bickering on the wire. Jealousy will also be aroused as neighbouring cocks attempt to court and feed their next door neighbours' wives (regardless of species) - and this may result in a severe beating of the fickle spouse by her husband.

Suitable Neighbours

Closely related and fightable species such as Port Lincolns, Barnard's, etc (regarded as within the scope of the Rosella group of parrakeets), members of the genus *Psephotus* (Redrumps, Blue-bonnets, etc) must also be avoided and only peaceable species sandwiched between. The most docile being the members of *Polytelis* (Princess-of-Wales, Barraband's and Rock Pebblers) or inoffensive *Neophema* Grass Parrakeets such as Bourke's or Elegants. These are followed by the more distantly related Kings *(Alisterus)*, Crimsonwings *(Aprosmictus)* and some of the Asiatic parrakeets *(Psittacula)* - Plum-headeds being the most suitable.

If larger Asiatics are used - such as Indian Ringnecks, Alexandrines or Derbyans - it is necessary to double wire the partitions between the flights; nesting activity will not be disrupted by these distantly related species, but even Indian Ringnecks - when they themselves have a nest or young to guard - will attack fledgling Australians on the wire and tear off their mandibles and toes; this I know to my cost.

Cockatiels make good 'separators' but for the fact that large nests of their young - fledging at a time when the parrakeets may have eggs or hatchlings - can panic in the middle of the night, and it is then that their flapping around will draw Rosella hens off their nests. Lightly coloured Cockatiels (being highly visible at night) are most likely to cause trouble in this respect.

Persecution of Hens

The seeming persecution of hens by their mates can be another worrying facet of breeding Rosellas for the beginner. Only experience will tell the aviculturist if the amount of chasing done to the hen by the cock is usual or if it is likely to end in a serious and grievous attack. Usually, the cock is satisfied when the hen retires to her nest, and this is his main objective, but something must be done if the hen is unreceptive to the cock and will neither take to her nest-box nor accept his offers of food; the most dangerous scene is one in which the chasing cock follows and corners his hen in the box in order to continue his attack.

Many hens have been lost in this way, usually suffering bites into the skull or damage and removal of the upper mandible. A few pairs are just completely incompatible, and cocks and hens must be split up and found new partners, in other cases the removal of a few of the inner flight feathers on one wing will slow down the cock's chase. If too many are pulled out, so that he is unable to fly at all, his breeding condition will rapidly deteriorate.

The cock's breeding condition may be brought on prematurely in winter by the stimulation of increased light when settled snow reflects the brightness of the sun; once again, this may lead to persecution of the hen.

As Pets

Rosellas are very active aviary birds, they are not really suited to cage life; if tame, as soon as they become mature, they develop a contempt for their owner and will take a spiteful delight in biting the hand that feeds them. They will learn to whistle short tunes and even mumble a squeaky word or two, but such caged pet birds are a travesty in comparison with their aloof aviary living counterparts.

6. *The Diet*

LIKE MOST PARRAKEETS, Rosellas are the easiest of birds to provide with a suitable diet; they are basically seed and plant eaters, and forage for their food in the wild amid tree tops and on the ground.

Seed and Grain

In the aviary they may be fed on the usual parrakeet mixture consisting mostly of: sunflower, (dry in winter as well as germinated in the breeding season), safflower, a little buckwheat, various types of millet (both loose and in spray), mixed canary seed (which includes hemp, rape and niger - care must be taken to see that the niger is fresh and shiny, not rancid), and a little wheat (green, dry or germinated in spring and summer). Oats, either dry or soaked and germinated, are another grain that some breeders find useful, but too much is very fattening and can cause a loss of general condition and deterioration in the health of the plumage.

If the birds will take it, maize is a good food (either whole, cut or kibbled, dry or freshly cooked), as well as fresh corn-on-the-cob. The smaller type of pine nuts are given by some breeders, but care must be taken to see that only the freshest and best quality pine nuts are used as this very oily seed can go rancid, and also attracts mould - as do peanuts and monkey-nuts. Birds have been killed by mouldy peanuts, and the mould is not always obvious until the shell is removed. Peanuts and monkey-nuts have also been known to cause constipation to the point of a blockage of the gut when fed to excess; if fed at all, only peanuts suitable for human consumption should be used, non-salted of course. Oily seeds like pine-nuts are also believed to interfere with the assimilation of calcium and are said to cause egg binding and even rickets in nestlings, if fed to excess.

Check samples of seed from several merchants if possible and give only the best quality available. Apart from making sure that it is free of dirt and mould and not discoloured, seed is best tested by cracking open and tasting a few kernels - it should have a nutty taste and not be dried up and bitter. Sunflower has been given a bad name as being fattening and unhealthy for parrots, but long flights help burn off excess weight, and are not human beings advised that sunflower oil products are a healthy food?

Some breeders provide sunflower in a separate container so that their birds do not kick out the entire contents of the seed dish in searching for their favourite items - usually sunflower and hemp. Much more seed is eaten in severely cold winter weather and should not be rationed, especially in our climate. Parrakeets can go through fads of preference for various foods as the seasons pass, and these fads should be pandered to when young are being reared in order to encourage and help the parents in the work of feeding their nestlings.

Germinated & Soaked Seed

Germinated and soaked seed helps stimulate breeding condition and encourages the feeding of young, but great care must be taken to see that it is only given fresh and contains no harmful moulds or infections; a few breeders give nothing else but soaked and germinated seed during the breeding season, others refuse to take the extra risk with their birds' health and stick to a dry seed mix.

Sunflower, hemp and millet are the quickest seeds to germinate; the seed should be soaked in water for a few hours during the day, drained off, rinsed thoroughly and left to stand by a boiler or somewhere warm overnight; by morning the seed will be showing white shoots and should again be rinsed thoroughly before feeding to the birds.

Only enough seed as can be used up and cleared away daily should be soaked at one time, so as to avoid passing bacterial, viral and fungal infection to the birds; fungal spores can invade both digestive and respiratory tracts, and also produce powerful toxic agents. In any case, once shoots of sunflower seeds have started to turn green they are bitter and unpalatable.

Soaked and sprouted millet sprays are a great favourite with most parrakeets, but they rapidly become stagnant.

Some breeders put a small amount of *calcium bicarbonate, calcium propionate* (a food preservative), *'Milton'* (for sterilizing baby bottles), or even some iodine based disinfectant into the water in which the seed is soaked, but it is best to be wary of using even simple chemicals in this way, especially when nestlings are being fed. Even so, in *'A Guide to Rosellas'* (published by *Australian Birdkeeper*) it is advised that *chlorhexidine* may be (quote) *'safely used in the water during the complete process'.*

American lovebird breeder Anthony Olszewski promoted the use of *calcium propionate* in the nineteen eighties. He recommended that seed should be soaked in water containing one teaspoon of *calcium propionate* per one and a half gallons of water. He also suggested it should be used for sprouting pulses, preparing chopped fruit and vegetables, and adding to Lory nectar; he used it in soft food and hand-rearing mixtures at a rate of one level teaspoon to a pound of the dry mixture in order to prevent souring in warm weather. Mr Olszewski also advised of the use of a small amount of *calcium gluconate* in drinking water as a preventive against egg-binding in hens and calcium deficiency in nestlings. I have given *'Calcium Sandoz'* (which contains *calcium glubionate* and *calcium lactobionate*) on whole meal bread as a preventive measure against egg binding; a hen which had become egg bound at the commencement of the season for two years running laid normally in subsequent years after being given a small piece of bread soaked in soya milk and a half teaspoonful of *'Calcium Sandoz'* daily for two weeks previous to laying and until the eggs were laid.

Greenfood, Fruit and Vegetables

A small but daily supply of greenfood (either collected from the wild or grown in the garden) is advisable for the birds' general health. Many breeders grow such foods as spinach beet, cress, etc specially for their birds and even encourage the flourishing of seeding weeds in the garden flower beds. Some breeders avoid giving too rich or too strong garden greens such as cabbage as they believe that it inhibits the assimilation of essential minerals into the birds' system; with Eclectus Parrots, which require a much larger amount of greens than Rosellas, breeding records show that large quantities of raw cabbage have been consumed even during the rearing of young, with no ill affect being apparent; however, caution is advised where parrakeets are concerned and only innocuous greens should be fed profusely.

Though masses of seeding weeds are a malediction for the serious gardener, their spring time crop is a benediction for the parrakeet breeder. Chickweed is always the first weed to appear and the quickest growing; in the greenhouse amongst the tomatoes, in the borders or in the vegetable plot; better than all the flowers in a garden to a bird breeder are great mats of seeding chickweed, but late cold springs result in a lack of this important food at a time when it is most needed. The tiny cups of milky white seeds are avidly sought out, but the juicy stems and leaves are also eagerly munched. If a dependable supply of this mild but nutritious plant can be found throughout the spring and a small amount given daily to pairs which are rearing young, their interest in keeping nestlings well fed is greatly increased.

Easily identified by its tiny white star-like flowers, chickweed can be found growing in gardens and allotments where earth has been turned in the previous autumn or winter, as well as in greenhouses - but care should be taken not to pick plants where chemical spraying or any kind of contamination may have taken place. If the weather is dry and the plants show signs of dehydration, the gathered chickweed should be spray washed and left to float in a bowl or bucket of water for a few hours (even over night) to freshen up, then drained off well before being offered to the birds. Do not pull up the whole root, and try not to pick all the chickweed from one place, but seek as many supply areas as possible so that each plant has time to recover and continue growing; try to keep the chickweed bed well watered to increase the chance of a continued supply into the summer. Chickweed and other green food should be given in the morning, so that the parents will be feeding it to their nestlings early in the day; if offered too late, in the afternoon or evening, the parents may fill themselves and their young with green food at the last feed of the day - instead of with more solid seed kernels, etc - and this is likely to cause scouring and death.

Just after the winter, when lush greenfood may have been unobtainable or withheld because of sub-zero temperatures, the birds should not be given large amounts, just a tiny sprig for the first few days, gradually increasing to small bunches; the sudden appearance of a large mat of chickweed, which they may not have been used to eating since the previous late summer, can upset their digestion, causing scouring, enteritis and death if they are allowed to make gluttons of themselves.

Beside wild picked greenfood, the presentation in the spring of more stimulating fare which will help awake the parrakeets' breeding instinct after the winter, also includes germinated seed (which is higher in protein and vitamin levels than dry) and soft food (bread and milk or canary rearing food).

With birds like Rosellas kept in outside flights the year round, during winter in freezing weather, anything of a high water content - fruit, vegetables, cooked food - should be given in small amounts only, to be eaten quickly before it freezes; the breeder should beware feeding greens to birds in outside flights in freezing weather; frozen fruit and greens often cause scouring. Warm boiled or baked potato and cooked pulses, are cheering in cold weather and some parrakeets will take small amounts of this kind of food. Likewise in winter, I often give the parrakeets a small spoonful or two per pair of birds of a 'pudding' made with wholemeal bread, cows' milk or soya milk, some sultanas, honey, peanut butter, a little *'Marmite'*, a sprinkle of vitamin/mineral powder and anything else they might appreciate - they waste a lot of it, but if they only take a little it does them good.

In freezing conditions, many breeders omit giving their parrakeets fresh water, saying there is no need because they eat ice and snow. So they will, but whether this is good for them is another matter, the absence of drinking water combined with low temperatures can quickly cause kidney damage. It is generally found that - as well as taking more food - parrakeets seek more water than normal when temperatures stay below freezing all day; when given warm water they go straight down and drink heavily. Though Rosellas are not prone to frost bite, in freezing weather it is as well to keep water levels in cups and dishes lower, so that their toes are not immersed as they sit on the side.

It is worth repeating that care must be taken to see that wild picked or garden greens are not contaminated in any way, by chemical spray, car exhaust, white or black mould, wild birds or domestic animals.

More greenfood - especially the usual wild seeding plants such as chickweed, dandelion heads, sow-thistle, milk-thistle, shepherd's purse and seeding heads of various grasses later in the season - should be available from the time when the birds are likely to begin nesting, and offered daily when they are rearing young. If the season allows, green heads of millet and canary grown in the garden or greenhouse can be given as a treat, though they are not always ready in time to help encourage nesting and rearing - apart for the autumn/winter breeding Northern Rosella.

Suitable berries and fruits collected from the countryside as soon as they become available are very much appreciated by Rosellas. In Britain our staple wild/garden berries are rowan, elder and hawthorn, occurring in that order of availability from late summer into the winter; pyracantha and cotoneaster berries are used by parrakeet breeders to a lesser degree but can be found in large accumulations right through the winter in some areas. Budding twigs of non-poisonous tree species such as willow, apple, silver birch and so on, can be given regularly.

Chopped apple, pear, orange and other fruit may be given regularly, and peas, grated carrots and sweet corn can be added to the mix. Though they may be refused, other vegetables, such as beetroot, swede and potato can also be offered (as they are to larger parrots) either raw or cooked as is appropriate for the vegetable, remembering that some raw vegetables may be toxic to a varying degree. Garden beans, such as runners, are often given raw without any apparent ill effects, but for safety should be cooked, as many types of bean can be poisonous to a varying extent in the raw state. This also applies to *dried* beans; as a precaution against any natural toxic content, after being soaked and/or sprouted it is wise to cook them for a short time.

Though many types of tropical fruits and vegetables can be used, it is especially advised *not* to feed avocado as it is believed to be poisonous to parrots.

Softfood

When young are in the nest, wholemeal bread with milk is an invaluable rearing food, and skimmed milk is probably better than full cream. It should be fed in very small amounts to prevent spoilage, and feeding commenced previous to the breeding season so as to accustom the adult pair to making use of it; sterilized milk does not become sour as quickly as fresh milk. Though bread and milk is a traditional and apparently successful rearing food, some veterinarians tell us that milk cannot be completely digested by parrots, and instead some breeders use soya milk which is eagerly accepted by parrakeets.

Canary egg rearing food can also be offered. Some breeders make their own egg food with hard-boiled yolk of egg, crumbled digestive biscuit, rusk, glucose, honey, grated carrot, crushed toasted whole meal bread, etc - all mixed up to a moist crumbly consistency and offered fresh. Soft food can be given two or three times a week, unless there are young being reared when it is likely to be eagerly consumed daily - at least in the initial stages of rearing.

Though it is not at all necessary to give Rosellas animal protein such as livefood, Rosellas do take insects and their larvae in the wild, and aviary birds have been seen eating earth worms (which can introduce internal parasites); one breeder mentioned the feeding of crispy bacon rind as a titbit.

Many breeders use a reliable vitamin/mineral supplement to sprinkle on the food, but a little goes a long way and too much can be harmful; some breeders stop giving these supplements once there are hatchlings and rely on a good varied diet providing all the essential nutrients. All the necessary vitamins and minerals should be provided by the foods mentioned; vitamin D - which is essential for the assimilation of calcium - is created by sunlight playing on the birds' skin and feathers. If birds must be kept inside without the benefit of sunlight, it is possible to purchase strip lights which are said to stimulate this vitamin D production.

Calcium and Water

Cuttlefish bone should be available at all times and is a good and easy way of providing the extra calcium which is needed for the birds' breeding efforts; it should be clean and white with no trace of dirt, oil or mould. To help avoid waste, open topped envelopes made of folded nineteen gauge welded mesh, wired onto the *outside* of mesh covered shelter doors, make good simple containers for cuttlefish and can easily be refilled from the feeding alley side when the cuttlefish has been gnawed away by the birds.

Grit, in various types, as a source of minerals and an aid to digestion is a traditional avicultural requisite, but recent suggestions believe its importance to have been over emphasised - certainly, a very small amount of gritty substance is required for the gizzard to do its work but a surfeit of grit consumed is harmful. Charcoal is often given along with grit, but now its use is being questioned, it is believed to cause depletion of vitamins - yet Australian psittacines are known to eat charcoal left from bush fires in the wild.

Some breeders believe that it is important to use only filtered water for their birds, even here in Britain, but others still find no harm in giving it straight from the tap. Fresh drinking water must be provided daily in a pan which is deep enough to encourage bathing, but kept shallow when young are fledging in order to prevent their drowning. Plastic or polythene water containers are better than those made of metal, they are easier to clean and easier to free of ice in winter. As soon as ice is removed from water Rosellas will be eager to bathe, even in the severest of weather. Contrary to the belief of some keepers, birds do not have the sense to avoid drinking their own bath water and so two supplies are not required!

Feed and Water Dishes

In our variable British climate, large cat litter trays have proved to be ideal as water dishes for medium sized parrakeets to large sized parrots, and these can be placed on the floor in the open flights. They are three and a half inches (89mm) deep, sixteen and a half inches long (419mm), and twelve and a half inches wide (317mm); they have rounded corners which make them easy to clean out with a stiff washing up brush, and being made of a pliable plastic material, they are resilient against frost as well as the sun. Only seldom have even large species been found to chew them, but if this should occur they must - of course - be removed immediately and replaced with earthenware, porcelain or metal dishes. It has been known for parrots to die as a result of crops and digestive systems being compacted with chewed up bits of plastic.

Occasionally some of these plastic trays get split or smashed when ice is removed in the winter, but - without accidents - they can do good service for ten years or more; they are very inexpensive to replace.

The seed dishes I have used for many years have been specially made from rivetted galvanised plate steel and are totally indestructible. They measure four inches deep (101mm), nine inches long (228mm), and five inches (127mm) wide. Two bands of metal are rivetted on one side and bent around so as to form two hooks; the seed dishes are hung inside the shelter feeding hatches at waist height.

The fasteners found on the tail gates of flat-bed commercial vehicles have been found to make ideal fasteners for feed hatches; they are mounted on a wide metal flange which guards against release of the catch by even the cleverest of parrots.

Where the food being offered is mainly fruit and vegetable, the acid content reacts with galvanised metal, and so it is safer to use receptacles made of porcelain, glass, plastic or stainless steel. To prevent these from being knocked to the ground, a tray with high sides can be easily made from heavy duty welded mesh; or the dishes can be lodged in metal hoops of the appropriate diameter which are bolted to the sides of the birds' shelter or mounted on the inner side of the door.

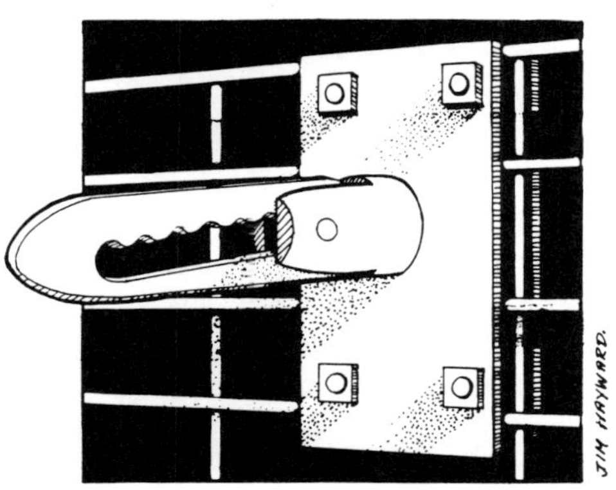

VEHICLE TAIL-GATE FASTENERS can be welded on sheet metal for bolting onto doors *(left)*, or on thinner galvanised plate for clinching over top and bottom wire mesh *(right)*.

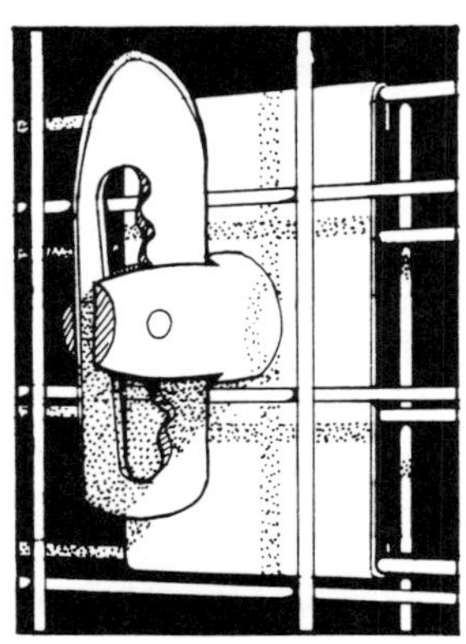

TYPICAL GARDEN AVIARY LAYOUT suitable for parrakeet breeders *(below)*, with flights arranged off sides of a central garden shed; the shelter/feeding area is inside the shed, and wire mesh covered walk-ways protect the occupants and allow for the owner's access without risking escape of the birds.

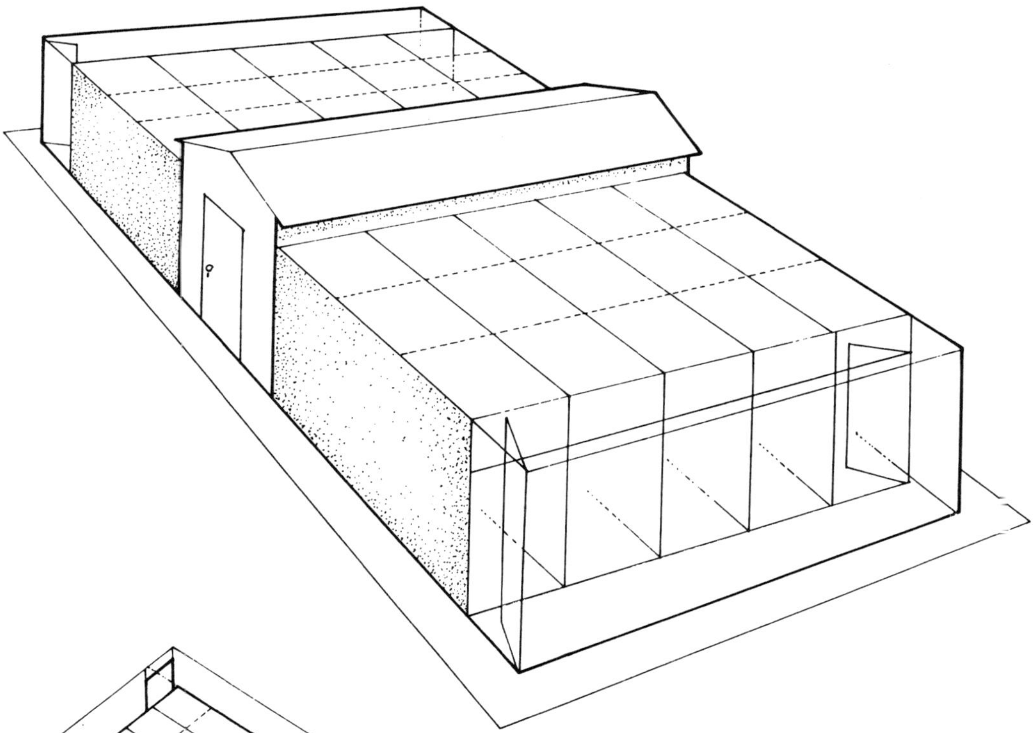

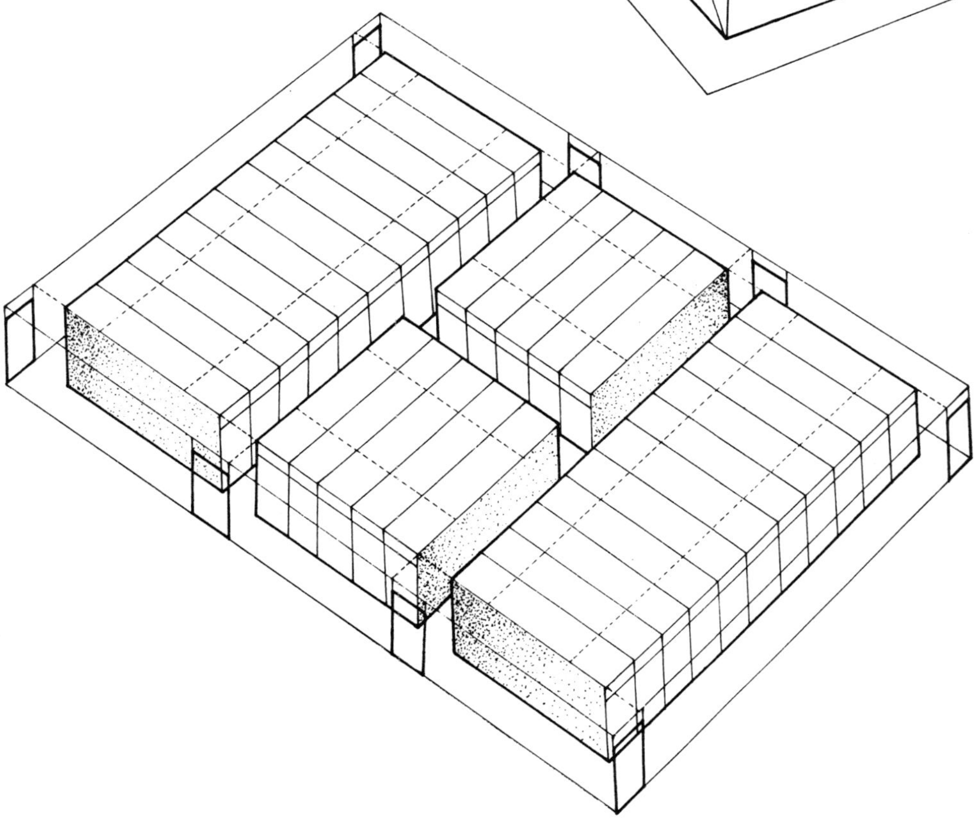

EXTENDED PROTECTED COMPOUND of aviary blocks *(above)* suitable for large sized parrakeets. Shelter/feeding areas can be situated whichever end suits the conditions and position of the aviary compound; the central 'H' layout of access and feeding alleys, ends of flights, as well as appropriate areas of the perimeter walk-way, can be roofed over with a translucent or a solid material. The sides can be covered in mesh to allow for sight of the birds from outside, or clad with either a translucent (plastic) or solid sheeting (board or galvanised iron) to afford the birds total seclusion. Well placed external doors make easy access for feeding, cleaning, wheeling barrows etc; further internal doors can be placed at strategic points within the aviary compound, to make it easier to catch and return escaped birds to their individual flights. In order to give clear access, some doors need hinging on the right, some on the left.

7. *Aviaries & Nest-boxes*

THE POSITION of the site for your aviary or - more likely - range of aviaries, must be given careful thought and consideration. Parrakeet breeding is an occupation that just keeps growing, and so it is unlikely that the novice is likely to be content with one, two or even three pairs of birds. Space should be allowed for extra shelters and flights to be added as and when required; the structure must be designed as simply as possible so that the joining on of extensions can be easily completed, and the materials which are to be used should be selected with this same purpose in mind. Uniformity in the dimensions is a great help, and it is best if these dimensions are divisible by a yard, or perhaps a metre. To a great extent, the area of ground available to the aviculturist will govern the choice of species which can be kept.

Both security and access are two very important points to think over. It is surprising to note that many breeders prefer to keep their treasured and valuable birds on the most remote part of their property, far away from their home; and, because they are considered unsightly, the aviary structures are often heavily screened off from view of the windows by trees, shrubs and evergreens. This is strange, apart from the fact that it should be a pleasure to be able to see the birds from the home, the most important aspect of security is easier to attend to if the aviaries are close to the owner's living accommodation; power points and mains water are also that much closer for any connections that must be made.

While considering access, the possible need to get into service alleys with a wheel barrow or hand truck should be allowed for - it can be very frustrating and laborious when refurbishing aviary floors to have to carry earth, sand or gravel back and forth in sacks.

Surrounding Vegetation

Heavy undergrowth shields interlopers from quick detection, and - while on the subject of surrounding vegetation - the possibility of poisoned birds through dangerous plants, shrubs or trees must be avoided. For example; perhaps the most common poisonous garden tree is the golden chain (*Laburnum anagyroides* and its cultivar *Laburnum vossi*). The flowers, seeds and roots are most dangerous, but no part of the tree is safe. Its poison is so deadly that it is said green food growing in close proximity absorbs sufficient poisonous substances from the roots to make it lethal in its own right.

Yew *(Taxus baccata)* is a common enough evergreen which claims the lives of both animals and humans from ingestion of its shoots, leaves and seeds; who would like to gamble that it would not be poisonous to psittacine birds? Softbills, especially thrushes, swallow its luscious red fruit, but the seed at its centre is passed out undigested in the birds' faeces - this would not be so with parrakeets which have muscular gizzards in their digestive systems for grinding seed and extracting all the nutrients which they contain.

It is wise to identify and check up on all the plants and trees around the aviaries, it is surprising how many are poisonous; even some common vegetables are poisonous if consumed raw - runner beans *(Phaseolus coccineus)* are one example.

Overhanging branches of even non poisonous trees can be a nuisance. Flocks of wild birds may take to roosting in them, spreading disease and both internal and external parasites to the aviary occupants; cats will be able to sit above the aviary and terrorise the inmates, while owls, grey squirrels and other wild creatures that are predatory to birds may also live and breed in a very old tree with spreading boughs.

High winds can send branches crashing down to pulverize shelters and flights; this danger is ever present with old and brittle species of such trees as crack willow *(Salix fragilis)* and the numerous types of elm *(Ulmus)*. Leaves may accumulate on wire roofs and, if left for some time, cause the wire mesh to rot prematurely - climbing plants should be prevented from spreading their tendrils throughout the structure for the same reason. The roots of trees can be equally as troublesome, distorting and pushing up foundations and framework.

The planting of shrubs and other plants actually inside the standard size parrakeet aviary is not advisable; the planting of shrubs would mean retaining an earth floor which increases the risk of internal parasites; keeping the floor clear of debris becomes difficult; foliage obstructs the view of the inmates so that sick birds may not be noticed; any foliage provides a harbour for infectious material; the bases of the plants provide hiding places and havens for mice - and the larger parrakeets will usually gnaw twigs and branches so that, in any case, the plants are gradually destroyed.

Fast growing non-poisonous evergreens are useful as wind breaks as long as they are not planted too close to the aviaries and kept clipped, and deciduous trees can be useful in providing shade against the summer sun as long as they also are not too close. When maximum light is needed in winter, bare branches allow it to filter through, in summer they will be in full leaf when the sun is at its highest. If mature trees exist on a property, the aviaries should be situated in a position which allows shade to pass over only a part of the flights, allowing the birds to shelter from the summer sun at the times they most need to do so - but leaving the aviaries bathed in sunlight in the early morning and late afternoon.

Two ancient species which are often despised are the May bush or hawthorn *(Crataegus monogyna)* and the elder *(Sambucus nigra)*, but to the true aviculturist these old country yokels are cherished. They have the advantage of not growing to tall, being hardy, long lived and also providing food at the end of the summer. Though more in favour as a garden tree, the mountain ash or rowan *(Sorbus aucuparia)* falls into the same category; some races grow more quickly and taller than others, and for this reason it is best to choose specimens which have been cultivated for use in the small garden.

Be warned that the dwarf elder *(Sambucus ebulus)*, which grows to just under a metre, is regarded as poisonous; it does not grow into a tree and its stems die down at the end of the year.

Position of the Site

The site for a block of aviaries must be in a situation that affords protection from predators, vermin and the worst excesses of the elements, so it should not be in an exposed position, but neither should it be down in a sunless hollow where fog or freezing conditions linger in winter. The aviary structure should be built with the protection of its residents uppermost in mind, and aspects of ornamentation should not be allowed to compromise the well being of the aviary occupants.

Shelter from blizzard and storm is best accomplished by cutting off the coldest winds from the north and east (in our northern hemisphere), but it must be remembered that the strongest and most damaging winds blow in from the west. Aviaries should not be built on the north side of a high wall or fence, which will place them in the worst of all positions, facing the worst of the winter weather while being in perpetual shade and never receiving the warmth of the sun; a southerly facing aspect is best.

Rats will travel in, along and beneath walls to gain entrance to aviaries, so an existing wall should never be incorporated into the aviary construction. The aviary should be built far enough away from any walls so as to allow for the excavation of a 'rat skirt'. A dry stone wall should never be included as part of an aviary; its honeycomb structure and the presence of the birds' food close at hand provide a self-catering holiday home for rats and mice.

If flights are built with their longest elevation facing the open, this vulnerable area causes torment to the birds as they are unable to retire to a safe and comfortable distance from humans or animals standing or moving about at the front of the aviary. It is best to have the narrow elevation facing outwards, and better still if the front is protected by a wire mesh covered passage, with the remaining three sides boarded up or filled in with corrugated plastic sheeting.

It is a bad arrangement to have flights situated close to an entrance, whether for traffic or for pedestrian use; the continual disturbance in the day and sudden flashing headlights at night will reduce chances of breeding success to a very low level. The powerful beams of automatic security lights in the wrong position would also have a disruptive effect on the birds. Access to the close vicinity of the flights to every occasional visitor should not be allowed. An enclosed area around the aviaries in which a watch dog or dogs can be given free run both day and night is ideal, and will help deter pests of both an animal and a human form. In country areas particularly, extra thought must be given to the problem of foxes, weasels and stoats.

For their own good as well as preventing the possible irritation to neighbours through the birds' calls, psittacines should be housed as far from neighbours as possible, in the centre of the property rather than against boundaries if this can be arranged. This could help save a great deal of aggravation from irate, intolerant neighbours, their dogs and their cats, and their children; balls and other objects landing on the tops of aviaries from the other side of the fence as children play can ruin a breeding season.

The site must be well drained and not prone to flooding. I remember the example of a bird breeder who had a waterway running along the back of his aviaries which was held at bay by a concrete block wall at times of high water. One very wet autumn the concrete barrier gave way and the aviaries were flooded to within a couple of feet of the tops of their roofs. To catch and save his birds the owner had to gain entrance by ducking beneath the water level and netting them as they flew to and fro just above the surface - all the while he knew that the water was rising and he could easily be trapped beneath the wire roof and drowned.

The positions of public service items and facilities which may need the attention of workmen pose other dangers to aviary birds. I recall an instance when a breeder lost several nests of young, eggs, fledglings and adult parrakeets which were terrified out of their minds when workmen had to clamber about up top of telegraph poles close by the aviaries. Nothing frightens birds more than something moving about or menacing them from above; on this occasion the workmen took several hours rearranging converging lines attached to a telegraph pole overlooking the breeding flights, and the birds were terrified into a state of exhaustion, with some beating themselves to death and all the eggs and young being deserted. Such seemingly unimportant, familiar objects such as street lights, and poles which carry electric cables or telephone lines would most likely be completely overlooked when laying out the site for a range of aviaries, but might be the cause of disaster months or even years later, so it is sensible to give some time to surveying the property thoroughly for these and other similar sources of nuisance.

Last but not least, it is important to make sure that no legal restrictions exist that will hamper your plans; if your property is rented or leased there may be conditions which stipulate that animals - including birds - cannot be kept on the premises. In some areas planning and building permission may be required, though in general, if your property is freehold and residential, no problems exist for wire structures and shelters which do not exceed two metres in height, and which do not cover more than fifty per cent of the ground area. However, it is safer to check with the local authorities if you are considering building an extensive aviary block where previously nothing has existed.

Avoiding Infestation of Round Worms

As already mentioned, Rosellas forage on the ground and this means that they are highly susceptible to internal parasites such as roundworms and threadworms. To eliminate the danger of losses due to the parrakeets' digestive systems becoming invaded by these pests, regular dosing with a de-worming agent should be carried out three to four times a year.

Experienced breeders dose their birds by means of a syringe and catheter tube introduced down the throat and into the crop; usual de-worming products in Britain include *'Nilverm', 'Nemicide'* and *'Panacur'*, but nowadays other de-wormers are sold which have been developed specifically to be administered via the birds drinking water; the novice should seek advice on de-worming from a veterinary surgeon who specializes in birds.

In previous decades the building up of large stocks of aviary bred Australian parrakeets was held back by heavy losses amongst the young of the year, especially during the autumn when roundworms would take their toll. After the first de-worming agents came into use, progress was rapid; before this time breeders were even resorting to moving their flights to fresh ground every year in order to avoid the accumulation of worm eggs.

Probably the best type of aviary floor to help in the prevention of worms is one in which the top soil has been dug out and replaced with a covering of small pebbles - approximately a half inch in diameter - which have been laid to a depth of between nine inches and a foot. On well drained land, the rain or a hose washes all sediment down through the stones; a periodic 'going over' with a garden fork or spade, followed by a hosing down, keeps the covering loose, and this also prevents mice from making nests. Of course, this small shingle will need digging out and replacing at some time - depending on the situation of the aviary, and the amount of action by earth worms.

Covered Roofs

Over recent years the complete or partial covering in of roofs has become popular as a way of helping prevent the introduction of disease and parasitical worms by wild birds, but this does not provide total immunity from the problem. Of course, if wild birds habitually roost on branches overhanging an aviary, the risk is great, but if the aviary is situated in an open area - which is best - the danger is minimal. It is important to keep roofs clear of leaves and debris, and construct them so that pools of stagnant water cannot form to make an ideal culture medium for harmful microbes - rapid and fatal diseases can be spread to psittacines when the 'microbe soup' overflows into aviaries.

Covered roofs are one way of preventing attacks and deaths due to panic caused by predators like cats and owls and even birds of prey such as sparrow-hawks, now that their numbers are on the increase.

A dog kept loose on the property is a reasonable deterrent against cats in day time, but many cat owners are completely anti-social as far as bird breeders are concerned, because they turn their animals out to sneak around all night being a nuisance. Cats dislike rain, but on moonlit nights they are at their very worst and can cause mayhem, resulting in the loss of eggs, and young and adult parrakeets, which ruins a breeder's season and quite often causes an aviculturist to give up parrakeets altogether. Remedies vary greatly, from running a conventional electric fence around the entire perimeter of the edge of the aviary roof - which works in keeping them off - to the more doubtful method of laying plastic bottles of water on the roofs, which is *supposed* to frighten cats away. Quite possibly other breeders have their own novel ways of dealing with the cat problem. Some breeders take the attitude of *'if you can't beat 'em join 'em',* and find that obtaining their own cat (the larger, more aggressive and blood thirsty the better) is the best deterrent, as it keeps rivals off its own territory - how frequently the animal turns its attention away from other cats and concentrates on the birds it is supposed to be inadvertently protecting is unknown!

Aviary access alleys should of course be covered in to provide shelter for the working attendant, and - if enclosed shelters are not used - the shelter end should be roofed over for five or six feet to give protection from the weather and keep the feed dishes dry.

The opposite end of the flight can also be covered over for three or four feet to give extra protection, and this provides another dry feeding area should a second feeding station be needed; for example, where hens are being persecuted by cocks and are in danger of being starved, or as a temporary measure to encourage youngsters to learn to feed more quickly.

Numerous materials can be used for aviary roofing: corrugated fibre, plastic or metal sheeting, or plywood with a covering of mineral felt are usual. The material can simply be nailed or screwed on to the top of the aviary framework; but it is better if a separate sloping roof framework is made to give a fall which drains off rain water, prevents standing pools and helps stop irritating drips. Agricultural grade corrugated metal sheeting covers a wider area, and transparent sheeting of the same profile is manufactured, solid and transparent sheeting can then be mixed as required.

Metal sheeting radiates heat onto birds sitting beneath it in hot weather, and frost forms on the upper and lower surfaces of all roof sheeting in winter. To provide additional insulation, roofs and shelter walls are often lined with plywood and painted, to make the interior lighter. However, lined partitions and roofs make ideal homes for mice which - once established in the hollows provided - are practically impossible to completely eradicate.

Repairs to roofs should be completed in the autumn after the breeding season and before the winter, not forgetting to shut the aviary inmates into their shelters or they will be terror stricken as the work of maintaining the wire and framework is carried out above their heads. Wire mesh loses its galvanised coating much more quickly on roofs rather than on sides and partitions and should be closely examined for patches of rust and holes. The protective layer of zinc on galvanised mesh can break down much more quickly in industrial areas, and the emission of corrosive gas has been known to cause holes in new mesh within a few months.

Where aviary framework is made of wood, its contraction and expansion over the seasons cause staples to gradually rise and these should be hammered back down and added to if necessary. It is important to make sure that aviary roofs are strong enough to take the weight of a heavy fall of snow - they have been known to cave in.

Making a Rat Skirt

If they gain entrance, rats can destroy all the inmates of an aviary in a single night, they will even attack poultry as they roost; young rats can be independent enough to survive while not much bigger than field mice, they can get through three quarter inch mesh (19mm) and - where there are hiding places - not be noticed until they have grown large enough to dig wide burrows.

To keep rats from digging into the aviary where the aviary framework is made of wood, make a 'rat skirt' by tacking onto the bottom runner a strip of sixteen gauge galvanised welded mesh (with apertures no larger than one inch by a half inch - 12mm x 25mm), measuring approximately two feet (.61m) wide; lay back the adjacent turf or dig a shallow trench and bury the mesh under it. Galvanised sheet metal can be used instead of mesh, and - where the aviary frame has been mounted on courses of bricks or concrete blocks - the metal or mesh can be tied in by being sandwiched between the first and second course.

If the aviary is surrounded with a buried skirt of mesh in this way the rats cannot bite through it, at least during a single night; sheet metal will be an impassable barrier. The sides of the aviary should be kept clear of any bits and pieces which vermin could hide beneath, they dislike working in the open and choose to dig their burrows under cover at night. Areas of cement floor should be reinforced with welded mesh because rats can gnaw through loosely mixed concrete; if the aviary perimeter is surrounded and abutted with a concrete path, the 'rat skirt' should be tied into this.

Foxes are now numerous in many areas of the country - urban as well as rural - and if these animals are prevalent in your district, a material which is impervious to their jaws must be used to clad the exterior perimeter sides and ends of the aviary or aviary block. Weasels are troublesome in many parts and their intrusion must also be prevented.

Mice are impossible to exclude, so, if they make an appearance, a routine of bait laying must be planned to destroy them quickly, with thought being given to the position of bait stations so that none can be carried into the birds - like wild birds and rats they are serious spreaders of disease. If it is your practice to put out food for wild birds during the winter months, remember to remove any surplus before nightfall as it will encourage rats and mice. Also, as has been mentioned, some species of wild birds - especially greenfinches, sparrows and starlings - are most susceptible to contagious disease and, for your kindness, may spread disease to your parrakeets if the feeding station is situated close to their aviaries.

MAKING A RAT SKIRT

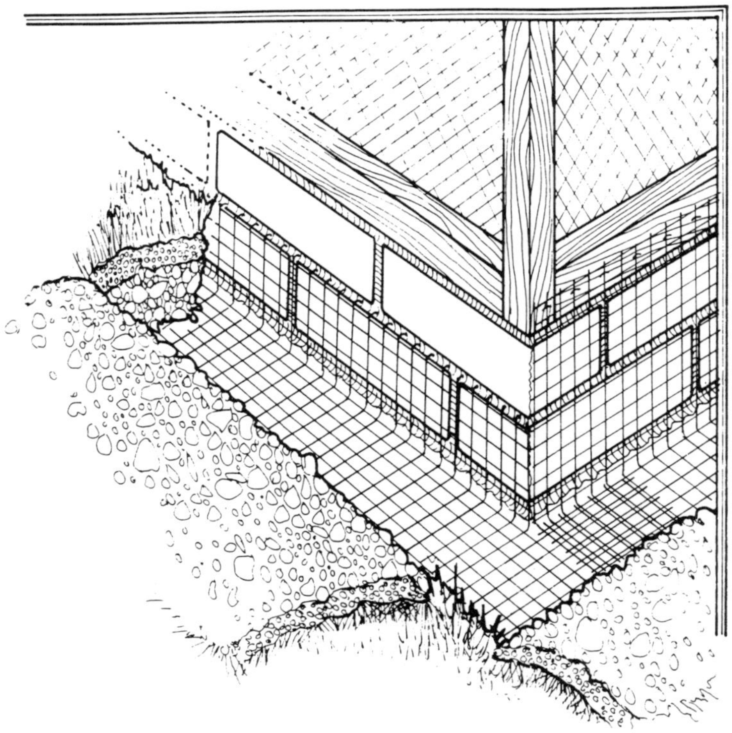

The Flights

Flights are usually arranged in rows with shelters and feeding places along the back and a service/safety alley both back and front. Flights joined end to end with a pathway along the front make birds nervous because they cannot keep a comfortable distance between themselves and the viewer; though often built this way in zoos and bird gardens, in order to keep as short a distance as possible between the visitor and the birds, this type of layout is impractical for most private breeders as it also wastes valuable space.

It is most convenient to have a suitably sized combined feed-store/first-aid shed attached to the aviary layout, ideally with electric laid on so that heat and light is immediately available for the emergency treatment of any sick or chilled birds.

It is advised that flights be at least fifteen feet (4.5m) long, six feet (1.83m) high and - for convenience of management - at least three feet (.91m) wide. The older generation of parrakeet breeders are used to providing extremely long flights for their birds, often thirty feet (9m) and even longer. The advantages are stronger fitter birds due to the additional exercise, and less overweight specimens, with a resulting improvement in fertility. The disadvantage is the danger of fatalities through broken necks and cracked skulls, caused by sudden impact at the far end of the flight when birds are panicked - especially at night and when youngsters are fledging. Leafy branches placed at the ends of flights help prevent this problem with fledglings in the day time, but at night time, danger to young and adult birds can only be overcome by shutting them in an enclosed shelter at dusk; this may not be convenient or advisable for other reasons, such as the possibility of pugnacious adults attacking each other or their young when in a smaller enclosed space.

Though not destructive to the point of fanaticism, the largest members of the genus are capable of chewing through very thin woven type wire netting and can easily escape, so this fact must be borne in mind when obtaining mesh for the aviary; the use of at least sixteen gauge welded mesh is advisable - with apertures no larger than one inch by a half inch (12mm x 25mm) to prevent small wild birds and large vermin wriggling through.

It is safer not to allow parrakeets into flights covered with new wire in case of zinc poisoning, but to wait until the brightness has been weathered off; alternatively, a mixture of vinegar and water swabbed over new wire is believed to effect a rapid 'curing' of the layer of zinc galvanising. Once galvanised mesh has been weathered for a season, it can be painted each year to help retain the sacrificial zinc coating for longer than would be normal and protect the underlying steel core from rusting, so giving the mesh longer life. Black bitchuminous paint is most often used, but other exterior quality paints could be considered once assurance as to their non-toxicity has been confirmed by the manufacturer. Water based emulsion paints should be avoided because they actually promote rust. A roller is more convenient to use than a brush and spreads the paint more quickly; the paint should be applied in thin coats to avoid globules which the birds might bite off, and be thoroughly dry before the birds are allowed into the flight. Likewise, when treating woodwork with creosote or *'Cuprinol'* wood preserver, make sure it is thoroughly dry before any birds are given access.

Enclosed shelters are best of course, but many British breeders find that open fronted shelters - with top and side cover - give sufficient protection. Though Rosellas can withstand freezing weather, they must be protected from strong chilling winds. The aviary must be situated so as to avoid this danger, or at least the wind baffled by hedges and fences.

The framework of the flights is often made with galvanised water piping jointed together, lengths of box metal section welded together at the corners, or *'Dexion'* coated angle iron lengths cut and bolted into shape, but aluminium and stainless steel is being used increasingly. If a wooden framework is decided upon, the fact that much of the timber available nowadays is already impregnated with preservative should be remembered, and enquiries made as to the likelihood of any danger of poisoning to gnawing parrakeets. Supporting cross members should *not* be fixed *inside* the flight roof; fledglings - especially - fly along the top of the roof taking the feathers off the tops of their heads, jutting cross members cause deaths through cracked skulls and broken necks. The exterior sides of the aviary block should be clad with corrugated plastic, cellular plastic sheet, corrugated metal sheet, weather boarding, exterior plywood, exterior chip board or oil bound hardboard, giving seclusion for breeding birds and protection from the elements and predators. Likewise, solid barrier partitions for four or five feet (1.21 - 1.52m) from the shelter end of the flight helps stop inquisitive or quarrelsome neighbouring birds causing interference to breeding birds.

Nowadays some kind of security alarm system is necessary; conventional alarms which work when a contact or beam is broken can be installed, as well as movement detectors, while video and intercom equipment is used increasingly. The traditional watch dog (or several dogs) is of course invaluable, and Chinese geese are sometimes used as natural alarms.

Perching

Many breeders prefer natural branches of fruit, willow or other non-toxic tree species for perching, or lengths of rough sawn timber, but three quarter and one inch (19mm and 25mm) diameter dowel rods are ideal and do not clutter up the flights as do odd shaped branches. To provide a good grip for the birds' feet (which is essential for successful mating) the perches can be spiralled with a deep cut using a sharp knife, or scored by dragging the teeth of a rip saw down their length. Perches need fixing firmly in a position which allows the birds room to mate; one perch at each end of the aviary, about a foot (.30m) from both the roof and the aviary end is sufficient and leaves maximum aviary space for the birds to exercise.

THE LARGEST SPECIES of *Platycercus* and *Barnardius* are sometimes given 'grand-father clock' nests when obstinately refusing to go to nest. Both upright *(left)* and sloping *(right)* 'grand-father clock' nest-boxes can be set on paving slabs **(1)** in order to retard rot. The welded mesh ladders **(2)** should be hammered and stapled well into the woodwork to prevent nails and toes becoming trapped. A perch **(3)** can be fitted beneath the nest entrance, or a batten **(4)** can be nailed across to give foothold. In the absence of aviary uprights to provide fixing points and give support to the sloping box, a prop **(5)** made with a piece of planking can be treated with creosote, planted in the shingle floor at its foot, and screwed to the underside of the nest, so as to provide stability. The best material for making nest-boxes is three-quarter or one inch (19mm or 25mm) marine/exterior quality plywood.

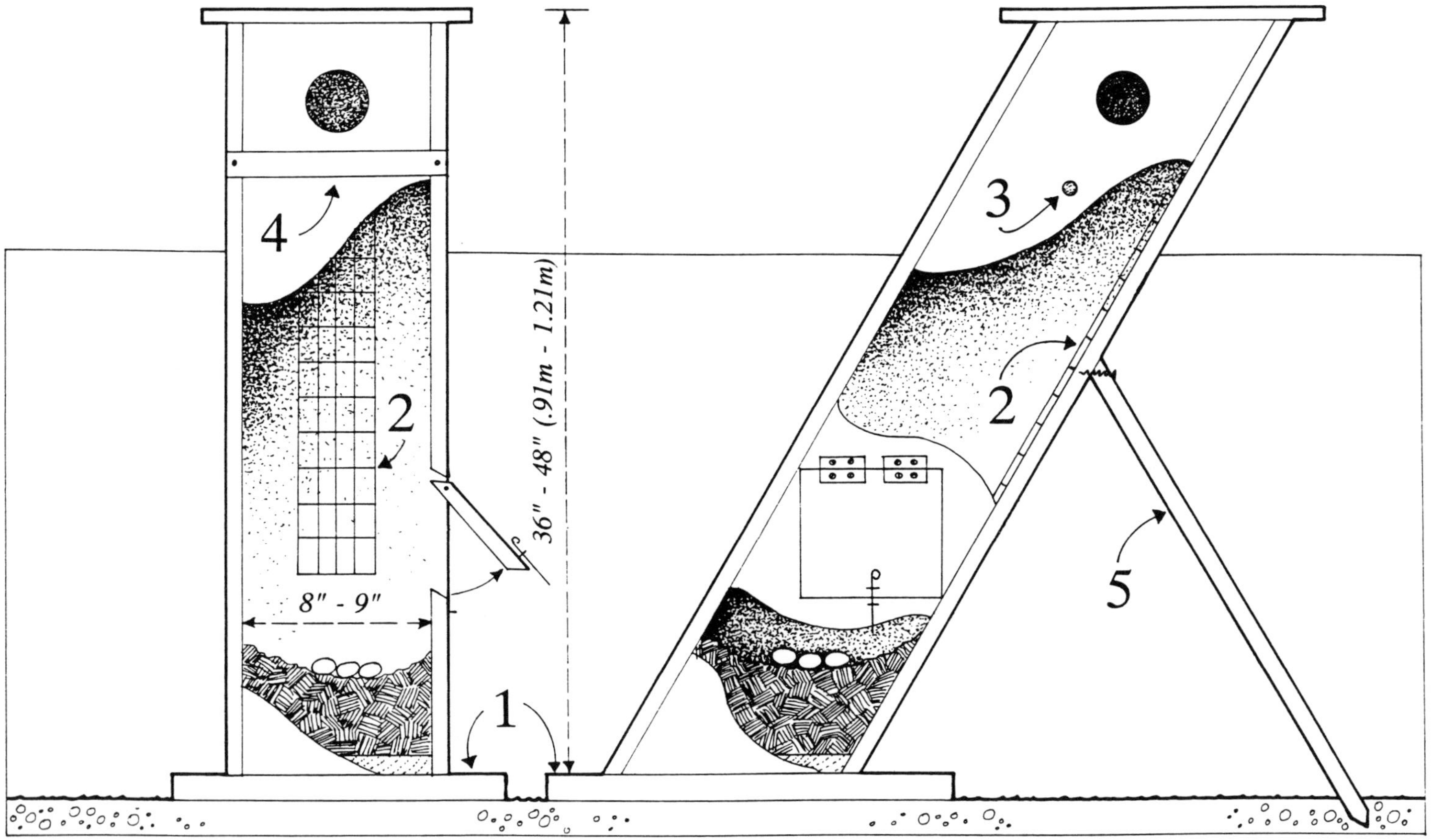

Nest-boxes

In cold climates - as in Britain - nest-boxes should be rather snug and tight fitting, helping the hen to keep the eggs or young safely beneath her warm feathers. In large boxes, eggs and young that roll away into far corners may become chilled and then perish. Many hens tend to stop brooding and return to their old roosting positions when their nestlings average just ten days old - so a smaller cosy box helps the young to conserve their body warmth and survive cool nights. This they do by clustering together in a circle with their heads hanging over each others shoulders, the larger youngsters on the outside with the smallest hatchling usually managing to wriggle into the middle of the heap.

In countries where exceptionally hot weather is normal during the birds' breeding season, larger more roomy nests are advised so that the young can separate, avoid close contact and get away from the body heat being generated by their siblings. It is best to use wood of around an inch (25mm) thick for nest-boxes, in order to give the best insulation against both cold and heat; some breeders go to the trouble of acquiring hollow logs, but the installation of such bulky and heavy objects can be a major problem.

The boxes we have used at Carterton Breeding Aviaries for Rosellas, and similar sized psittacines, are made of exterior quality three quarter inch (19mm) or one inch (25mm) plywood, and measure seven inches (178mm) square inside by fifteen to eighteen inches (381 - 457mm) high. So as to make a better access for the hen, and one which helps protect against cracked eggs as nervous birds scuttle into the nest, those set up for Rosellas are fixed at an angle of thirty degrees from the vertical. The entrance hole should be snug fitting for the species for which it is provided, and have no sharp or jagged pieces sticking out that could damage a hen full with eggs. A piece of welded mesh stapled and hammered into the inner face of wood (so there is no danger of nails or toes getting hooked and birds becoming trapped) just below the entrance makes a suitable ladder. Internal slat ladders made of wood can be gnawed through and fall on eggs and young.

Nests are best fixed under some cover, not in the open flight where the sun may bake the occupants or the rain wash in to chill or drown them.

Suitable Nest Filler

A covering for the floor of the nest to a depth of two to three inches (50 - 76mm) is made up of a mixture of crumbled well rotted wood and sieved soft sand. It is a good idea to lay some logs, branches or old pieces of timber under the hedge in a dank corner every now and then, so as to maintain a constant supply of rotted wood for nesting material. Peat is often used as a nest filler, but as it drys out it becomes dusty and can cause hatchlings to become asphyxiated; fresh mixed wood shavings from a timber yard might contain resin or preservative which is poisonous to parrakeets, or could give off fumes which would kill hatchlings in the confines of a nest-box.

Turf Base

The old method of ramming a cut turf in the bottom of the nest presents a risk; as the hen excavates the turf, small sharp stones can be dug out and these will easily puncture the eggs. Thoroughly soaking the turf bottom and interior of the box used also to be a regular practice, but in low temperatures a wet nest is a cold nest, and in higher temperatures a wet warm nest is an ideal medium for the growth of harmful bacteria, mould and other organisms.

Some breeders simply provide a wooden concave (as with budgerigars' nests) but this does not satisfy a hen Rosella's strong instinct to dig over and arrange the interior to her own liking. To avoid disturbing nervous hens it could be better to place the nest (under cover) at the opposite end to the feeding area.

Treatment of Nest-boxes

Many breeders are very fastidious about the treatment of the nest-boxes at the end of each breeding season; the box is removed from the aviary, the old filler tipped out, the box is thoroughly washed out, disinfected and - when dry - creosoted inside and out, and then stacked under cover until the next breeding season.

Using creosote or any other wood preservatives on nest-boxes must be questioned; if badly soiled, it is safer to scrape out the inside and sterilize the inner (and outer) surfaces and corners by giving them a lick over with a blow lamp. If not in too bad condition, it is only necessary to remove the top layer of floor covering and replenish with a fresh scattering just before the next breeding season. Nest-boxes can be left in position over the winter as long as the entrance hole is closed up with a square of thick plywood, not only to prevent the hen becoming stimulated into attempting breeding out of season, but also to make sure that the box is totally sealed against mice.

The re-hanging of a nest at the beginning of the season is regarded as being an added stimulation for some pairs, but - conversely - others seem to take a while to get used to its reintroduction and are more confident to use it when left in position the whole year.

Some breeders routinely add a little insect/mite powder to the bottom of the nest at the beginning of the season and between broods, others regard this as being a source of positive harm to the hen, eggs and young.

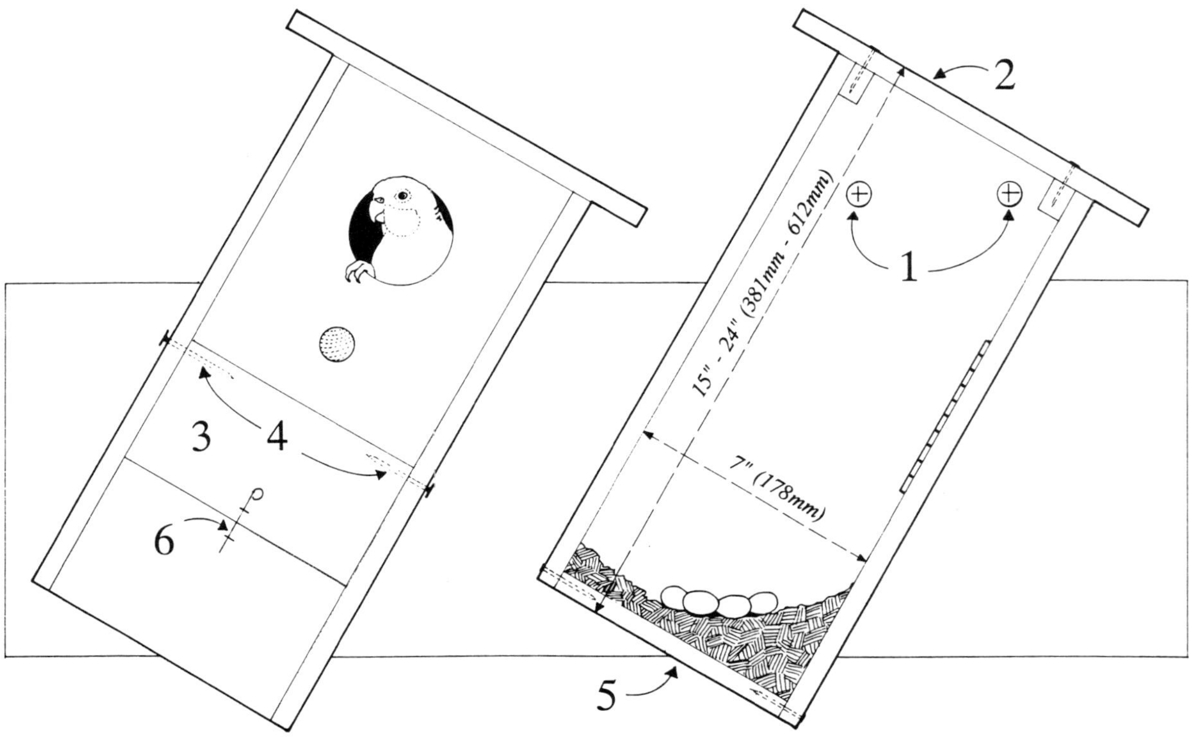

HANGING NEST-BOXES can be screwed (**1**) firmly to the aviary structure at an angle, to prevent nervous hens dropping straight down onto eggs. To make cleaning easy, both a removable top lid (**2**) and a side inspection door (**3**) are needed. The door can be hinged by inserting two pivotal nails (**4**) which pass through the sides and into the door flap; top and bottom edges of the door should be cut at outward sloping angles to prevent ingress of water. The nest bottom (**5**) should be cut so that it can be fitted and nailed *inside* the walls of the nest, again to stop water leaking in. A wire pin (**6**), dropped through a staple on the door and a staple on the face of the nest, acts as a fastener.

8. *The Breeding Cycle*

THE IDEAL SPRING weather for Rosellas is wet and warm, this provides plenty of chickweed and discourages early moults which result in a complete loss of breeding condition. Warm showery weather which continues into early summer increases the likelihood of second broods. Unseasonal hot dry weather in April carrying on into summer causes exactly the opposite and can result in a lost breeding season. Mild winters do not necessarily herald good breeding years, Rosellas can become confused with no clear demarcation between winter and spring; an incoming warm, damp spring after the fog and frost of a hard winter is a good stimulus for the nesting instinct.

Management

It is wise to make some rules about the management of your birds before the commencement of nesting activities. Once an adult breeding pair are established in their quarters, do not move them any more prior to the breeding season, nor any birds close by, unless such a disruption is absolutely unavoidable, such as fighting, or birds becoming ill. Also, if you have empty flights adjacent to breeding birds, the commencement or period of the breeding season is *not* the time to go buying extra stock with which to fill them; much better to leave them empty in readiness for weaning those youngsters which it is hoped will be produced. Visitors should be banned from the aviaries and adjacent area; the attendant should not loiter about for too long, but stick to a strict routine regarding feeding and cleaning and give the birds as much seclusion as possible - even so, an eagle eye must still be cast swiftly over the stock and aviaries both morning and before dusk for potential problems.

Once nesting is under way, extensive major cleaning operations to the aviaries must be curtailed, only a basic routine of clearing up should be carried out and this done quickly with the minimum of fuss; for example, removing stale food to prevent infection, sweeping up of spilled seed and husks which encourages mice, and washing away of the birds' droppings. By the way, do not be surprised to see your birds eating their own droppings, this is a normal occurrence from which they are thought to gain benefit by topping up the natural 'flora' of their digestive systems; it will do them no harm as long as they carry no infections or parasites and the faeces are either fresh or totally desiccated and free of mould.

Sexing by the Wing-stripe

As has been mentioned elsewhere, sexing is only sometimes possible by the row of spots on the underwing, referred to as the 'wing-stripe'; but its presence or absence varies depending on the species, sex, and age of the individual.

In the Eastern and Mealy Rosellas the wing-stripe is absent in adult cocks, usually present in adult hens and present in immatures of both sexes. In the Brown's Rosella the wing-stripe is absent in both adult cocks and adult hens, but usually present in both sexes of the immature bird. In the Pennant's and Adelaide Rosellas it is absent in adult cocks, generally absent in adult hens, but present in both sexes of the immature bird; while in the Yellow and Tasmanian Rosellas it is absent in adult cocks, usually present in adult hens and present in immatures of both sexes. In the Stanley Rosella it is usually absent in adult cocks, but present in adult hens and both sexes of the immature bird.

In Barnard's and Cloncurry Parrakeets it is absent in adult cocks but present in most adult hens and immatures of both sexes; in the Port Lincoln and Twenty-eight Parrakeets it is absent in adult cocks, most immature cocks and most adult hens, and present in immature hens. In the Pileated Parrakeet it is absent in adult cocks but present in adult hens and immatures of both sex. Other characteristics usually give a good indication of the sexes of members of these three genera, and it is unlikely that surgical sexing or DNA sexing should need to be used, accept in a minute number of cases.

The Breeding Season

In the cooler climate of northern Europe, the Rosellas' breeding seasons vary little between each species, commencing from as early as March to as late as June. Breeding hens that are double brooded may go down for a second nest as late as July or August, but if they are not inclined to do so they can drop into their moult as early as July. Hard working pairs may stall their moult until as late as October. Dry spring weather sometimes has the unfortunate effect of putting a stop to the birds' breeding condition and bringing on an early June moult which results in the loss of a complete breeding season; I have never known a hen Rosella to go to nest immediately after moulting.

If the weather is warm and dry just prior to the breeding season - and also if the dry spell continues into the breeding season and hens show no sign of nesting - it is a good idea to lightly spray the outside of the boxes and the aviary floor every day. This often promotes breeding condition and interest in the nest. Some breeders go to the trouble of installing a sprinkler system through the open flights which can be used to simulate rain showers; a hose - with holes at appropriate distances along its length - is run across the roof of the aviary block, attaching this to a tap which can be turned on as required provides the simplest method.

Australian species nest when conditions are favourable for the growth of enough food to rear their families, and dry weather makes this unlikely. Therefore a humid atmosphere, and the daily presentation of fresh grown seeding green food (chickweed is the most favoured) and germinated seed will persuade the birds that the time is just right. If spring is unusually cold so that chickweed is sparse, a greenhouse or cold frame can be used to grow some on until sufficient can be found.

COMMON CHICKWEED *(Stellaria media)* is a valuable food, especially for nesting birds.

The Northern Rosella is an exception to the usual spring breeding pattern and insists on nesting in late summer and autumn. Even so, in recent years, some pairs have also shown an interest in spring breeding. The reason for this may be the fact that European stock, in years past, was subject to hybridization with other spring breeding Rosella species - specifically the Eastern and the Blue-cheeked. Over the years the appearance of hybrid features may have been almost completely extinguished, but an indecision about whether to breed in spring or autumn may be the lingering result, with some exceptional cases of pairs breeding both in spring and autumn.

In earlier days, some members of *Barnardius* were notorious for missing the breeding season if prevented from nesting in the earliest months of the year, but nowadays spring breeding seems to be quite normal.

The Onset of Breeding Condition

The first sign that Rosellas are coming into breeding fettle is shown when the cock begins to chase the hen up and down the flight; he is usually the first to inspect the nest, gingerly peering into the entrance hole as if something might jump out and grab him. He immediately shows his excitement by spreading and swinging his tail rapidly from side to side - chattering as he does so. This draws the hen's attention and, after a few nervous false starts, her curiosity overcomes her and she ducks inside.

I have found that no birds will enter a nest-box which has a large amount of spiders' webs cris-crossing its interior, and these should be thoroughly cleared away before allowing the birds entry; like humans, parrots hate to get clinging webs over their faces. Taking into account the existence of poisonous spiders in Australia, a wariness of *arachnids* must be inherent.

During the days that follow, the hen will be seen to be less afraid of the cock and accept his offers of regurgitated food with increased confidence and trust. She begins to spend more time in the nest, digging over its floor covering and altering it to suit her own liking by carrying and kicking out some of the material through the entrance hole. It is best not to have the litter in the box too deep as the hen's instinct to dig may result in the burying of eggs.

UNRIPE HEADS OF SEEDS are ideal for encouraging breeding condition and as rearing food. Even millet and canary can be grown in England, as is proved by this sample bunch which shows an amazing variety; all grown by accident from self-set seed laying between cracks in a concrete block floor, after an aviary was taken down.

The Nesting Cycle

Rosellas usually lay from four to six eggs, though further on some exceptional examples of large nests of eggs and young will be given. The eggs are laid every other day and incubation commences on the second or third, so that the first couple of young to hatch are several days ahead of the last to emerge. After about five days of incubation the beginnings of a formation of red veins can be seen if the eggs are 'candled' with a strong torch light, but it is not advisable to interfere with the nesting birds to carry this out - each egg hatches after an incubation period of eighteen to nineteen days. While checking for fertility, first make sure your hands are not smelling of scent or pungent materials; eggs should be handled as little as possible, and not at all in cold weather; light bulbs should not be used for candling in case of overheating the egg. Clutches of eggs which all seem to be 'clear' should not be thrown out too quickly, with a late sitting hen the first eggs *might* be infertile but the last laid could still develop embryos; the same goes for late hatchings - many a breeder has felt like kicking themselves on opening up an egg thought to be dead-in-shell which is then found to contain a live embryo.

It is unwise to inspect the nest when the hen is inside, she is almost certain to jump up and scold the intruder, and in doing so often scatters eggs or hatchlings against the sides of the nest-box, causing them serious damage. If inspection is carried out, remember to replace the lid or inspection door securely, forgetting to do this may seem impossible, but it is not and can result in the loss of all the eggs or young.

A STRONG TORCHLIGHT is quite adequate to check for fertility. The first signs *(left)* look like a faint cross floating within a fine circle of blood. After a few more days of incubation a network of veins *(centre)* forms rapidly, and the air space becomes defined. Almost ready to hatch *(right)*, the chick shows as a dark mass and the air space becomes greatly enlarged. Obviously, candling and checking of eggs presents a risk of breakage, desertion, dead-in-shell, and introduction of infection.

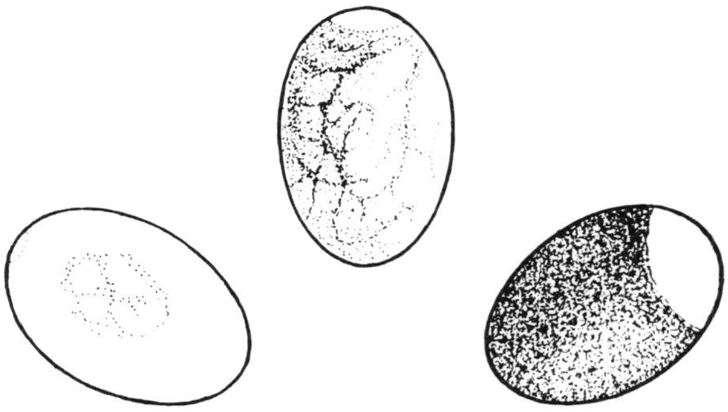

Problems with Eggs

Soft shelled eggs can be the result of breeding with immature hens and also indicates the lack of sufficient calcium and/or vitamin D3 which helps assimilate the mineral into the bird's system. If an egg breaks inside a hen, death is usually rapid. However, if the birds have a continuous supply of cuttlefish bone and sunlight to play on their feathers and instigate the manufacture of vitamin D, and provided immature birds are not rushed into breeding, problems with the making and laying of eggs are unlikely to occur.

Egg binding can be caused by depletion of calcium, a sudden cold spell which gives the hen cramps, by an awkwardly formed or rough egg, and sometimes by an extremely large egg. The affected hen is found in a collapsed state, breathing rapidly and in obvious discomfort; in order to save the bird no time should be lost in placing her in a hospital cage, or something similar, which will provide comforting warmth of eighty to ninety degrees Fahrenheit; a little warm olive oil can be run down inside the vent; hens full with eggs must be caught and handled with extreme care and not constricted. Some late hatched immature hens could be subject to egg binding if encouraged to nest too soon. As mentioned elsewhere I have used *'Calcium Sandoz'* in the prevention of egg binding.

'Calcivet' (Vetafarm) is a more recent product which I have not tried; it contains vitamin D3, calcium and *borogluconate* which carries the calcium across the gut wall into the blood stream; typical bird diets are said to contain plenty of phosphorus, so, although this is needed in the absorption of calcium it is not included in this preparation - the makers say too much can be harmful; they claim their product can *prevent* egg binding if given as per the directions. The makers advise it can be given to hens that are egg-bound by dropper into the mouth, straight into the crop with a syringe and catheter, or via a crop needle (gavage needle).

It is not a good idea to interfere with nesting hen Rosellas at all, and certainly not at the time when eggs should be hatching; novice breeders are so eager to see the hatchlings, and concerned that they may be overdue and have difficulty clearing the shell, that attempts at helping them are given; eggs which are only just 'pipped' must be left to hatch by themselves, frequently a hatchling parrakeet will take two days or more from first 'pipping' the egg shell to emerging - if it is 'helped out' before the yolk sac has been completely absorbed it is almost certain to die.

Outside interferences - such as night fright, storms, flashing lights, cats, and so on, which can bring the hens off the nest in the night or early hours of the morning, as well as interference from children, casual visitors, dogs, etc in the day - can cause 'dead-in-shell' and desertion of young. Seclusion is more important than is generally realised, and nest inspection by over anxious breeders - especially in cold weather - also causes a great deal of dead-in-shell as well as deaths of hatchlings. Another frequent mistake which causes death of the embryo is the wetting of eggs and nest by the attendant in the expectation that this will aid hatching - all it does in our climate is chill the eggs and unsettle the sitting hen. In attempts to breed Rosellas in inside accommodation without access to outside flights, the absence of *natural* light also plays its part in causing infertility, egg binding and dead-in-shell.

Hatchlings

On hatching, Rosella young are covered with a white down and look like the fluffy seeding heads of dandelion plants. They grow quickly, and by the time quills are sprouting have acquired a grey secondary down. The youngsters can be heard squeaking for food a few days after hatching; once their eyes are open and they are feathering up, any interference to the nest will set them all squalling in protest.

The hen broods her young for decreasing periods through the day as they begin to quill up, and - as has been mentioned previously - she will often cease to brood at night when the oldest is from ten to fourteen days old. When this occurs it is quite useless to catch up the hen at dusk and return her to the nest, as she will only fly out again after a short while. Under no circumstances should she be blocked into the nest with the young over night, in her panic and attempts to get out, the young can be killed. In any case, under normal circumstances and providing the young number three or four, their own combined body heat will sustain them through a cold spring night - as soon as dawn breaks one of the parents will go inside to warm and feed them.

Depending on the species, the temperature (which affects the growth rate) and the depth of the nest-box, here in Britain the young fledge at between just under five weeks to as long as six weeks. They are usually very wild and erratic for the first few days, blundering into objects, making their ceres bleed, and even scalping the feathers off the tops of their heads as they fly up against the aviary roofs. If the aviary is grassed, any long undergrowth should be cleared before fledging, and only very shallow water containers placed in the flight - this will prevent chilling or drowning of youngsters in rainy weather.

It is important that the young birds should be subjected to the very minimum of attention by their owners until they have acquired their full confidence and flying powers; even so, it is best to replace them in the nest for the first couple of nights after fledging - beyond this time they will usually shoot out within a few minutes of the attendant leaving the flight. Soon they will be roosting together in a row alongside their proud and attentive parents.

The breeder must watch for persecution of the young by the adult cock; this does sometime happen, especially if he is intent on driving the hen down for a second nest. Even though they may still be seen begging for food, the young are independent of their parents from three to four weeks after fledging - sometimes earlier - and at this time may be weaned and administered a de-wormer. The breeding pair should also be dosed against worms at this time.

As weaning flights for groups of youngsters, well sheltered, secluded aviaries should be provided, with plenty of feeding stations and bunches of millet sprays hanging by perches. For the first few days - well before dusk - their crops must be checked to see that they are full or at least partially full, in case they have not fed themselves and need to be returned to their parents to be fed. Young Rosellas have a nestling feather which is - in most species - much paler or duller than that of their parents; they moult in the autumn and acquire a transitional plumage. Even before this time they can be sexed by the size of their heads and bills, with the cocks being more bolder than the hens. I have bred with one year old birds from Easterns, Golden-mantleds, Stanleys, Mealies, Adelaides and Yellow Rosellas.

Ringing

Though the method of ringing a nestling is described here, it does not mean that I strongly *advise* breeders to ring their birds! It is of course a common practice with easily bred cage birds and serves to identify individual specimens where a breeder holds a large stock, but all breeders will have had experiences where birds have been maimed or died as a direct result of being fitted with a ring; apart from this - in many cases - the disturbance caused by the breeder to the nesting birds when fitting rings on youngsters can cause the nest to be deserted or young to be killed. Ringing the young of large species of parrots and parrakeets in the nest is a tricky job and not only entails the risk of desertion, and squashed and mutilated young, but also a good chance of the attendant getting severely bitten by the irate parents!

It is easy enough to ring birds that are being *hand-reared*, but nowadays some - if not most breeders - do not want to produce *only* hand-reared specimens, because their value as breeding stock is being brought into question; this attitude towards hand-reared specimens is certainly true of many experienced breeders of the Rosellas and their close relatives.

Apart from getting hooked up with rings and dislocating their joints, strong jawed parrots can squash a ring into the leg, cut off the blood supply, cause swelling, inflammation, infection and necrosis. We are told we should use tougher metal to withstand the pressure of the birds' bills - but I wonder if the people advising this have ever tried to remove a solid steel or brass ring from a large, frightened parrot whose leg has swelled up to such an extent that the flesh covers the ring on each side? If the metal is hard enough to withstand the strongest bill, it is unlikely that it can be removed with small cutters, and the only option left may be to have the actual leg removed by surgery.

Some parrot species - especially South American - have extremely short bones at the point where the ring sits between the foot and the first joint of the leg, and this can cause deformation. I once tried ringing a batch of hand-reared Queen of Bavaria's Conures many years ago; as they matured they all became irritated by the rings and began working away at them; some developed a deformation in the leg through the ring, all of them worried at the rings continually, gnawing at them until the engraved figures were obliterated, some crushed the metal into the flesh of the leg, while others even bit their legs with frustration because they could not remove them - in the end I had to cut off most of the rings myself.

If the practice of ringing or marking *all* birds in some way is just accepted, without it being pointed out that *not* all species should be ringed, there is every likelihood that the relevant authority will eventually *insist* that all foreign bird species *must* wear closed rings, as they did with our native British species. This is likely to lead to a situation where breeders will have to choose between breaking the law when they keep or sell birds which do not carry rings, or losing the young of species or individual pairs which are hard to breed because of attempting to ring them. A situation like this could lead to some people - maybe a substantial number - ceasing to breed birds altogether.

Novices must be warned about the difficulties resulting from the ringing of birds; however the actual fitting of a ring is easy enough. Firstly, the hands must not carry traces of any pungent odours which can be transferred to the young birds - oil, paint, tobacco, chemicals, soap, perfume, and so on - and should be rubbed in dry nest material before handling the youngster. Ringing can take place when the nestlings are from seven to ten days old; some young grow at a faster rate than others and may even be larger than normal at hatching. Rosellas' feet - like all psittacine birds - are arranged with two toes pointing forward and two back, so the front toes are passed through the ring, which is slid over the foot and up the leg over the two hind toes - these are then flipped out with a pointed match stick. The toes and foot may be moistened to allow the ring to slip over easily, but on no account should the ring be forced on when the feet have become too big, in this way tender flesh can be split and torn, and joints dislocated - it is better to try the ring while the nestling is smaller and if it slips off replace it a day or so later.

Foster Parents

Rosellas will of course rear the young of the various members within their own and closely allied genera, but sometimes they are willing to raise less closely related species. A pair of our Yellow Rosellas were used as foster parents for Amboina Kings; after sitting her full time, the hen Rosella's own eggs were examined and found to be clear, so a chance was taken and they were replaced with three Amboina King eggs. She continued to incubate and hatched the King's eggs, showing remarkable patience by sitting for a total of six weeks in all. The young were reared, even though they filled the nest to excess and dwarfed their foster parents.

Alternatively, it may be necessary to foster the eggs or young of Rosellas. In this case the most commonly used and most reliable species must be the Redrump. These hard working little parrakeets will rear their own youngsters along with fostered Rosellas as large as Pennant's. I have even added more foster young to the nest when some of the Redrumps had already fledged, and carried on adding more youngsters as the oldest foster Rosella became feathered. Cockatiels can be tried in an emergency, I have known of an exceptional pair that reared a nest of Blue-cheekeds, but there is generally a lack of willingness for this species to rear other than its own kind. Kakariki Parrakeets are also good feeders while the foster young are in the nest, but have been known to turn on Rosellas and kill them when they fledge - obviously mistaking the much larger youngsters for interlopers. Cotswold parrakeet breeder Alan Oliver has had mixed results with his foster pairs of Red-fronted Kakariki, one pair reared young Pennants from the egg to fledging, but once the young had left the nest they mistook their giant foster children for invaders, attacked and killed them; even so, other pairs have reared Pennants and other Australian parrakeets to full independence.

KAKARIKI PARRAKEETS are often used as foster parents, with mixed results; they are easily sexed, the cock has a much larger bill and head than the hen.

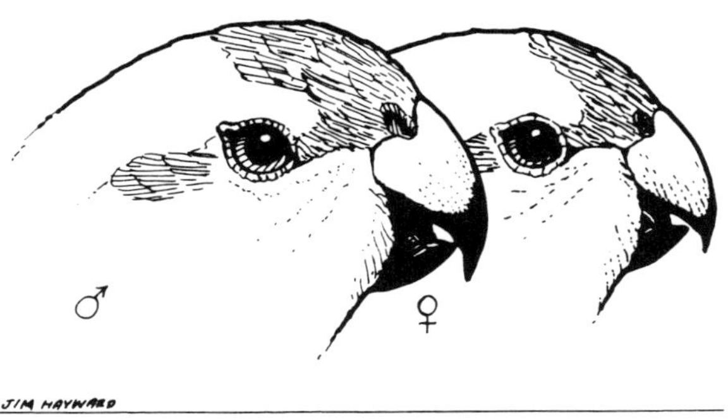

There are written reports of Rosellas laying prodigious amounts of eggs; one hen Pennant laid twenty-nine eggs but refused to incubate. Cockatiels hatched twelve of these but refused to feed them; four were placed under another pair of Pennants but died; only one egg placed under a pair of Barraband's - whose eggs were clear - was successfully reared. In another example, a hen Pennant laid a clutch of fourteen eggs but broke seven, two were addled, and three were placed in an incubator, in the meantime the hen was given some dummies until she became well and truly broody. When the eggs were pipping they were returned to the hen and she hatched and reared three youngsters. Two eggs were given to a pair of Yellow-fronted Kakarikis making their first breeding attempt, both hatched and were raised to independence.

Provided they are only slightly damaged, cracked or chipped eggs that have to be transferred for fostering can be repaired with a couple of coats of ladies' clear nail varnish; this is very often successful and the egg can develop and hatch normally so long as no microbes have gained entrance.

If an emergency arises where it is found necessary to hand feed the young until foster parents are available, Rosella hatchlings of only a few hours old will eagerly suck food from a small teaspoon, but it must be very warm. There are several brands of hand-rearing mixtures on the market especially for psittacine birds, but various types of food for human babies (which are available from the local chemist) can also be made use of; a dry powder variety which has to be mixed with boiled (not *boiling*) water is ideal, such as those sold under the brand names of *'Milupa'* and *'Robinsons'*, those types with the higher protein content for the youngest human babies should be chosen. A small amount of *'Wysoy'* (soya protein milk substitute) can be added to the baby food, and some breeders advise that a little apple sauce mixed in helps digestion.

Artificial incubation and hand-rearing has been turned into a science, with several books dedicated entirely to this subject, but a simple method is quite often adequate. The young parrakeets must be fed enough times through the day as will keep their crops from becoming totally empty, but not bloated and tightly distended. It is necessary to feed very young birds several times through the night, but older birds can be fed at about midnight and then left until six o'clock in the morning for the first feed of the day; they should be fed a further four or five times throughout the day. The nestlings must be kept warm and dry, their droppings are much more watery when being hand fed, and warmth is needed to maintain the digestive process and promote growth; hatchlings need to be kept at ninety degrees Fahrenheit (thirty two degrees Centigrade), so a small thermostatically controlled brooder is needed until they are old enough to be kept at room temperature. The older the parrakeets are at the time hand feeding begins the more likely they are to be successfully reared.

Exceptional Breeding Results

The loss of a cock Rosella just prior to the breeding season may not always result in the loss of its hen's production for that year; unconventional methods do work, if rarely, and I have run a cock with two hens in the past by allowing him into one hen's breeding pen in the morning and the other's in the afternoon; when the young hatched, the cock fed one hen through the wire.

In nineteen ninety-two Mr Ward reported in the *Parrot Society* magazine that his hen Golden-mantled Rosella had laid thirteen eggs in one clutch; three eggs were taken away because it was thought the hen would not cover them - but ten *did* hatch! One hatchling died when it was two days old and then the adult hen also died, but the cock continued to raise the rest of the brood on his own. The youngsters soon began to overcrowd the nest so they were transferred to a bigger box which was placed on the floor of the flight; the top of the box was only partly covered with a piece of wood to allow the adult cock to enter and continue feeding his young, which he did. The last of the fledglings stayed in the nest six days longer than its siblings, but one of its older nest mates returned to the box every night to sit by its side.

One breeder of Stanleys reported his hen laying a clutch of eleven eggs; the nest was made from a section of apple tree and measured ten inches (254mm) in diameter by thirteen inches (330mm) high - nine young were reared to independence. A year later on - in nineteen eighty-nine - *Parrot Society* member Mr Roger Everard topped this with his pair of Stanleys which went to nest in mid April. The hen laid ten eggs in a nest-box ten inches (254mm) square; by the twenty-fourth of May the whole clutch of ten young had hatched and, though there must have been a considerable difference in age between the first and the last hatched, all ten fledged towards the end of June over a period of only two days!

9. *Obtaining & Selling the Birds*

IN BRITAIN, licences to sell members of the three genera covered in this book are *not* required at present, *none* are on the UK Department of the Environment's Appendix I of endangered species, but *all* are on Appendix II, and licences are needed to export them.

If your new birds are obtained from the same specialist breeder it is likely that they will be slightly related; I believe that slightly related stock is acceptable with small to medium sized parrakeets and often makes up more stable breeding pairs than totally unrelated specimens, but *do* make sure you are not pairing brother to sister. Under certain conditions inbreeding is used by knowledgeable breeders, but it is not advised that beginners should start off in this way. A young pair of Rosellas which will 'grow together' are usually preferred over an adult pair, but adult pairs are fine as long as they are compatible, and you are sure they are not being sold because they have proved to be of no use as breeding stock. Just after the breeding season - from late summer to autumn - is the time when the biggest surplus of Australian parrakeets becomes available in Britain, so this is the time when there should be a greater choice.

With all species covered in this book, hens are almost always in slightly shorter supply than cocks, and so it is important to obtain a *definite true pair* at the outset. It is a bad practice to obtain odd birds - especially cocks - and hope to make pairs up at a later date; the longer adult cocks are left on their own the more aggressive they tend to become, and then they are very difficult to pair up. An over aggressive cock can ruin a potentially good hen; once a hen has been attacked she is nervous and extremely reluctant to approach another cock to be fed, and it may take a long time for her to overcome this reticence.

Purchasing the Birds

Before the birds being purchased are caught up - while discussing their attributes, faults and general management - stand back and observe them for a short time, make sure they are not drowsy, but active and strong flyers and watch to see how they react to each other if they are a pair. Rosellas do not engage in mutual preening like some other parrots, and tend to keep a safe distance from each other unless they are actually engaged in courtship, nesting and rearing, when feeding of the hen by the cock takes place; but, take note of little signs in their behaviour, such as the cock continually persecuting or trying to corner the hen, and any signs in her appearance showing that he *has* caught and bitten her, or pulled feathers from the back of her head or neck.

Look under the perches at the condition of their droppings, and those of any neighbouring birds; watch to see if they sneeze and have runny nostrils, or are continually rubbing their eyes on the perch - which are signs of disease. When the parrakeets are at rest, notice if they are continually pushing their heads into their feathers, shaking their heads, looking dozy, sitting with body feathers continually ruffed out, if their tails pump heavily, and their bills gape slightly as they breath - which could indicate congestion of the respiratory system.

Once a bird has been caught up, the purchaser should be offered the opportunity to hold each bird for a close examination: check its nostrils and eyes (look for discharge which indicates an infection, or white spots in the pupil which could mean the bird is blind or partially so); examine the feet, make sure they can grip, and check if any toes or nails are missing (some breeders will not purchase a bird lacking any nails in case it is unable to copulate, but I have bred with cocks lacking nails and even with one which lacked a leg!). Check the bill for damage, the vent and undertail coverts for signs of wetness and dirt which could indicate disease, the breast to make sure that it is well fleshed and that the keel bone does not stick out like a razor; examine the feathers for signs of distortion and biting, feather disease or external parasites; a few pin feathers just mean the bird is in the moult, but if it is *heavily* in the moult, preferably, it is best left until most of its new plumage has grown.

Choose birds for breeding that are bright of eye, clear around the nostrils, clean around the vent, lively, wary, but not terrified and in a state of panic when viewed in their flight, but - for my preference - not hand tame. Look for birds that are obviously feeding well and - if you *must* buy birds from inside a shop - not being kept in a high temperature. Find out exact details of their diet and keep them on this until they are settled in; if it is necessary to make changes to the diet, introduce these changes gradually.

If the purchaser already has experience in keeping other parrots, the knowledge gained will of course help in recognizing a decidedly ill looking bird from an apparently healthy one; nevertheless, always isolate any new stock for at least four weeks (some breeders nowadays recommend *six* weeks) to make sure that possible infections cannot be transmitted to the rest of your birds. If obviously sick birds can be seen at the premises from which purchase is intended, remember that those appearing healthy could soon develop these same symptoms. Remember that *sick* birds should *never* ever be purchased, however cheap; but if you are not concerned about *minor physical defects* that will not hamper breeding, also remember there should be a reduction in price for such birds. If you are not satisfied with the birds' appearance, leave them where they are; this is better than changing your mind later and then taking the birds back for a refund, it is not fair to the birds or to the breeder, who may be concerned about taking birds back into his aviary which - even during the short time away - could be bringing an infection back with them.

Settling in New Stock

It is best to collect the birds yourself rather than have them delivered, we have all received birds by rail or road at some time with which we have been disappointed, and may have been angry enough at being tricked to send them back, but, really, we have only ourselves to blame for buying them sight unseen.

Rosellas, or any psittacine bird for that matter, should be transported *one* to a compartment in order to avoid damage through fighting - even the most compatible birds may attack one another if suddenly placed together in close confinement. A completely enclosed box is *not* suitable for transporting birds and can be a death trap in warm weather, even with numerous air holes drilled through - one side (at least) is best half filled with mesh. Nowadays, purpose built small size animal carrying boxes made with a plastic material are becoming more frequently used.

When collecting birds by car, do *not* place the box in the boot, if the sun is playing on the back of the car in summer it will soon become excessively hot; if the body work of the vehicle is not too good, exhaust can seep in and finish the birds off very quickly. It is best to place the birds on the back seat, supported so as not to slide off and loosely covered with a light cloth which - on a long journey - provides nervous birds with seclusion, while allowing air to pass through as well as sufficient light as will allow them to feed if they wish. Some seed should be scattered on the floor, but water is not necessary, some pieces of juicy fruit will supply enough moisture. As much information about the birds as possible should be gathered from the vendor, especially what food they are used to, and enough to last for a couple of days should be obtained if possible so that everything is made as familiar to the birds as it can be.

Though your new acquisitions may have been kept in outside flights all their lives, a long car journey will warm them enough to make it dangerous to move them straight out into an open flight - even in mild weather. I have known new owners to arrive home late in the day or evening and turn their birds straight out into an unfamiliar aviary; their crops may be empty, they have no idea where to find the food dishes or a secure roosting place. So, after a chilly night probably spent hanging on the wire of the flight, they are either found dead or close to death from exposure and weakness through lack of nourishment.

It should be common sense to get the birds home as soon as possible with no unnecessary stops on the way. Provided they have not come from a warm environment and are used to cold or cool conditions, initially, they are best placed in flight cages of suitable dimensions situated within an unheated building. If they *have* been kept in a heated artificial atmosphere - which is unnecessary where *healthy* Rosellas are concerned and should bring uncertainty into the purchaser's mind - then a slightly warmer temperature than they have been used to should be provided, and gradually reduced over the following days or weeks until it reaches an appropriate level.

On introduction to their new accommodation, they must be given water with the chill taken off, but only sufficient to provide drink, not enough as would encourage bathing. If the birds soak themselves late in the day and go to roost still thoroughly wet, they are in danger of becoming chilled. A light should be left burning for the first few nights of their settling in period, so that the birds will have the opportunity to feed all through those night hours when they are left undisturbed. Once a normal feeding pattern has been established, the light can be left on for a diminishing amount of time until it is dispensed with completely. Your new parrakeets should be kept on the diet they are used to, until they are firmly established, after which gradual changes can be made if thought necessary.

Each parrakeet should be housed separately over this short settling in period, so that - during the daily cleaning out and feeding routines - it can be checked that they are feeding sufficiently, and that their faeces are healthy in appearance. Separation also prevents bullying in their restricted living area. It is wise to isolate and quarantine all new stock away from your established collection for four weeks or longer, to make sure that no infectious complaints are laying dormant to flare up and be passed on to your healthy birds. Always make sure that new birds have been recently de-wormed by their previous owner - if not, do so once their condition is satisfactory.

Introduction to the New Aviary

After undergoing this period of settling in and quarantine, introduction to their new breeding flights should take place on a suitably mild and quiet day for the time of year. A number of temporary food and water receptacles should be fixed by the perches at several positions for a couple or so days, until the birds have become used to their new surroundings, after which one feeding station should be sufficient if they are being housed one pair per flight. Sometimes, one partner of a pair may be domineering, and in this case two feeding stations set well apart are preferable. The birds should be let into their new quarters in the morning, but only after they have already had time to consume enough food to give them a start to the day.

Before dusk, the food should be checked to make sure that a fair amount has been eaten by the new birds, if there is no sign that food has been disturbed, they must be returned to their previously established quarters for the night, once more with the light on until they have fed. For those left outside, a further check must be made after dusk to confirm that they have each found a cosy roosting position - either *under* shelter or in an *enclosed* shelter - safely away from rough weather and predators. Because they generally prefer to roost at the highest point, shelters are often made higher than the flight to encourage the birds to roost inside.

Selling the Surplus Birds

It is important to maintain as detailed records as possible on the parrakeets in your aviaries for future reference, for example: when and where they were obtained, if ringed, ring markings, when de-wormed, any problems with health, occurrences and results of each breeding season of each pair; in the event of the loss of a bird, its age and cause of death; if sold, exchanged or given away, when, and the name and address of the recipient. Most breeders in Britain sell their parrakeets by advertising in *'Cage & Aviary Birds Magazine'*, *'Birdkeeper Magazine'*, the magazine of *'The Parrot Society'* or even local newspapers. If breeding is successful, birds are sold, and this continues yearly, then it is possible that income tax will be incurred; therefore it is important to save all bills and invoices which relate to *every* expense involved in the production of the birds sold - aviaries, food, stock, veterinary bills, etc - so that it can be set against tax due.

Plenty of advice is given regarding the purchase of birds, but little on the tricky aspects of selling birds. As far as possible, the customer is always deemed to be right, but there are a few out to take advantage of a person's good will and breeders must protect themselves as much as possible against such happenings - never more than with livestock. Here are a few tips - for which I have paid in the learning - for dealing with prospective customers you may never have met before.

It is always best and fair for the purchaser to see and buy the birds at the vendor's premises rather than have them sent by road or rail, when things can go awry; if the vendor is persuaded to send them by rail, it must be made clear that this is at the purchaser's risk and expense. Any physical defects should be pointed out clearly to the purchaser, this will save arguments afterwards; the vendor must make sure as far as possible that the bird is healthy and shows no sign of illness such as those described elsewhere in this book; the bird should have been recently administered a de-worming agent to make sure it is clear of these parasites. Only claim to sell birds of guaranteed sex if you are perfectly sure of their gender, if not, make it clear that they are being sold *sex unknown*. After catching up the bird, display it clearly to the purchaser and offer it for examination before placing it in the travel box. If the purchaser is a novice, make sure that he/she knows how to take care of it, the routine for settling in, and knows of any drawbacks with the species, for example, if it is likely to be noisy, needs a special diet, is destructive, if it requires heat in the winter, is aggressive by nature, suitable or unsuitable as a pet (if that is the purpose for which it is required), unusually difficult to breed (if breeding is the aim), or you consider it too rare and expensive for an inexperienced beginner.

If you are dealing with beginners who want to buy expensive birds, try to persuade them against purchase and suggest to them those species which are suitable for novices; never sell birds to children. Discourage any ideas that the bird is *sold on approval*; do not unconditionally guarantee the bird for *any* length of time after the purchaser has left your premises with the bird, there are many ways a bird could be damaged or lost through the purchaser's incompetence; make sure the purchaser has a suitable transport cage/box for the bird and that it has food and fruit sufficient for the journey.

Never allow birds to be taken away on the strength of an uncleared cheque, request cash for an immediate sale and warn a prospective customer of this condition before they make the journey to your premises; be prepared to give enough food for a couple of days, and also a written receipt. Be wary of the prospective purchaser who starts questioning a previously arranged price; never consider a bird sold until money has changed hands, we have all seen those advertisements, *'Due to time wasters, I still have the following ....'*. Beware persons who suddenly lose interest in the bird they were desperate to buy, and are more interested in seeing the rest of your birds, the lay out of the aviaries, your security arrangements and alarm, want to know if someone is always on the premises, if you have a guard dog, a shotgun . . . . . !

Seriously, if you are just getting started in the business of selling the parrakeets you breed, most interested people will be straight forward enthusiasts, but do not be bowled over by apparent enthusiasm and praise for your stock, retain a healthy reserve of scepticism and even suspicion about persons you have just met. But above all this, keep in mind that *the future welfare of the birds you are selling is of paramount importance,* and clearly outline the responsibilities of bird keeping to complete beginners.

10. *Health & Sickness*

IF THEY ARE well fed, correctly managed and suitably housed, Rosellas will remain in fine condition and good health. A most important rule for the beginner, and perhaps even more important for the person who already has a large collection of parrakeets, is to obtain new birds from a healthy and reliable stock, and isolate new acquisitions for at least a month (some advise six weeks) before introducing them into the same block of flights or area of accommodation as existing stock. It must be said that there is more chance of introducing infections and parasites into an established stock of birds if purchases are made from premises where the inmates are forever being changed or added to indiscriminately. Purchasing birds from individuals who are continually complaining of losses or disease among their stock is naturally to be avoided at all costs.

Early Symptoms of Sickness

Apart from birds which have been physically damaged in some way, the first signs of many illnesses are often the same and so give little indication of their cause. Those birds which are obviously sick will show their discomfort by continually ruffling their feathers, so as to trap more air and increase the amount of insulation against the cold; if the birds' environment (inside or out) is excessively warm this trait may not be apparent. Weakness may be seen in their movements and flight, and they may be unable to roost on one leg - as is quite usual.

A bird which goes to roost in the evening with both feet on the perch, just facing forward without its head tucked into its feathers, is definitely suspect. Half open eyes give cause for concern, normally when the eyes are blinked the action is rapid; eyes that close and open again slowly - giving a dozy appearance - indicate advanced deterioration in the bird's health. Lethargy is another indicator; a parrakeet which has a shy and timid nature will fly off to the farthest point in the aviary at the approach of an attendant, while a bold or a confiding specimen will come forward to satisfy its curiosity. If both types of bird disregard their owner's presence and are not alert to the movements of other parrots around them, then they should be carefully studied from a distance - so they are not aware of the watcher - in case they are in need of immediate and swift attention.

It is important for the attendant to become completely familiar with the personality and habits of each and every bird under his or her supervision, only then will health problems in their primary stages be quickly recognized. In this way many unnecessary fatalities will be avoided. There are so many little pointers that can aid in the detection of troubles on the way.

For example: as the food dishes are being replenished, the birds may come forward immediately when they would not usually do so; they may be seen to be drinking more than usual and sitting on the edge of the water dish for long periods, or picking over the food without actually consuming any. A favourite roosting site, occupied for many weeks, months, even years, may suddenly become vacated and the bird discovered in an unsuitable position. The normally dominant partner of a long established pair may suddenly allow itself to be intimidated by its subordinate, and chased away from the food supply. There are so many seemingly trivial incidents that may strike a note of discord in the attendant's mind and cause question whether all is well.

First Aid

Speedy action and first aid is essential if a truly sick parrakeet is to be saved. Though in the end there may be very little wrong with the suspect bird, where the health and safety of our charges are concerned it is better to be safe than sorry. I would rather lose the produce of a pair's breeding season than risk losing the bird itself. How often I have heard, *'It doesn't look very well, but I think I'll wait and see if it gets better',* and later, *'I lost that parrakeet you know, I wish I'd taken it into the warm - I'll never be able to replace it now!'*

The very basic requirements of a sick bird are: warmth, light, drinking water (tepid, not cold) and tempting food - in that order. It is wise to have ready either a small room or a well insulated shed fitted out with suitably sized cages and a thermostatically controlled heater, so that a temperature of eighty to ninety degrees Fahrenheit can quickly be reached and maintained for as long as is necessary, even in the depths of winter. A light should be kept burning throughout the hours of darkness for sick birds, so that they may feed and drink at will.

Sick parrakeets are often dehydrated and show great thirst, in this case it is easy to initiate a course of oral antibiotics if required; veterinary help and medication should be considered if a warm environment does not bring about a fast and positive response. Even so, it may be necessary to wait for a short while to see if there are any indications as to the nature of the problem before administering drugs.

Dosing or feeding via a catheter tube and syringe carries certain risks, even at the very best of times, and these risks are multiplied many fold if either is attempted with a weakened subject. If this type of treatment has to be resorted to, the parrakeet should be allowed to gain as much strength as possible in its warmer environment before being handled again - or it may expire simply from shock.

Warmth and drink are of more immediate importance than solid food, glucose may be added to the drinking water so as to provide the bird with enough energy to aid its recovery. I have known large psittacines to fast for several days before returning to solid food, as if they were resting their internal organs and allowing their natural functions to clear the digestive system before going forward.

As the health of the patient improves, the heat can be reduced by a few degrees each day, as long as the subject appears bright and tight feathered at this lower temperature. If other birds are in the room and still require a high degree of warmth, the temperature can be lessened for an individual by placing its cage at a lower level, while those most in need of heat can be fixed nearer the ceiling. Alternatively, some breeders use separate infra-red lamps to achieve the same result of differing temperatures for individual birds at various stages of sickness and recovery.

When previously housed in an outside flight, once a parrakeet has been taken inside - depending on the time of year and weather conditions - it may not be possible to return that specimen to its usual accommodation for several weeks or even months. In effect, it needs to be re-acclimatized.

A parrakeet that refuses food during an illness, just like a human, may need a little tempting, and it will be useful to know what items that particular bird favours above all others. It could be a little bread and milk, millet spray, grapes, peas, even livefood such as mealworms - anything that will revive an interest in feeding. Rosellas can usually be coaxed with a few tips of seeding chickweed or shepherd's purse; the tiny seeding heads of *Poa anua* grass can even be found in the midst of winter beneath snow - these bland plants are seldom refused and are not purgative in their action, provided only a small amount is given. In frosty or freezing weather any greenfood must be allowed to stand in the warm for a while before being offered.

Handling Large Parrakeets

Even if the attendant does not have tender hands, large parrots can inflict painful cutting bites, so it is important *not* to give them a chance to fix their bills into your flesh; grasping feet with needle sharp claws can also inflict deep punctures in hands and fingers. A glove that is thick enough and strong enough to withstand the pressure exerted between the mandibles of large parrots is so unwieldy as to make manipulation of the bird impossible; it is important to learn to handle your charges with your bare hands and without the help of another person.

The best tool to use in handling large parrakeets is a net with a hoop about twelve inches (304mm) in diameter with a padded rim to prevent damage when a bird is being caught; the bag of the net should be deep enough to prevent the bird from wriggling out when the hoop is turned on its side. There should be enough room inside the bag for it to be twisted around to secure the enclosed bird without constricting it. The material of the bag should not be a mesh material, but a strong cotton or linen cloth with an open weave sufficient to allow air through; it should be coloured dull green or brown - not white or any bright colour. The hoop must be firmly fixed on the handle which should be about fifteen to eighteen inches long (380 - 457mm); long enough to give enough reach to catch a bird but not too long as will make its use awkward in a flight three feet (.91m) wide.

An old dull coloured jacket should be worn when entering the aviary, one so old as to look as if it could find its own way around without human help is ideal. In a flight with a length of fifteen to twenty feet (4.6 - 6.10m), the attendant may stand in the middle of the flight and reach out to the bird to be caught with the net, this usually makes it try to fly past, and as it does so the net is swivelled open so the bird flies straight into it. If it does not fly past, the net is dropped over the bird; catching should be done quickly without chasing and exhausting the parrot, and without swiping at it as if a game of tennis were in progress.

By easing open the net a little, the position of the bird can be seen and then its head can be grasped (through the net) between the thumb and second finger, with the index finger over its crown; it can be held against the attendant's chest with the palm and arm. If the bird is to be taken from the net, this can be done with the other hand, the bird rearranged after the net is discarded and the bird's wings enclosed under the forearm.

If the bird is too large to be restrained in this way, the ball of the thumb may be slipped under the hollow beneath its lower mandible - with care taken not to exert any pressure in the region of the wind pipe.

If the legs are allowed to kick free, while struggling the parrot will sometimes fasten a claw into its eye lid or the skin beneath the lower mandible - in this case it should be released before it can tear itself. Never let go of a parrot until you are certain it is not gripping your hand or finger with a foot, otherwise it may turn and bite when released - let go of the bird gingerly and move the hands away quickly.

For the simple purpose of moving a bird from one flight to another in the same aviary block, it may be driven into the service alley and guided into the new flight without catching it. When moving birds from one block to another, it is best to transfer them from the net to cages in case the attendant trips and they are released back to the wild inadvertently.

Examining the Bird

A quick examination should be made of the bird as it is caught up, because this will avoid further stress and upset being caused by having to catch and handle it again after having released it into the warm cage. Make a note of such evidence as discharge from the eyes, nostrils and/or ears, and crusty deposits around the same areas. A runny eye could be a sign of something simple like a slight abrasion, or could raise suspicion of the possibility of an infectious disease. A cheesy exudate inside the nostrils and ear holes, and white lesions inside the mouth indicates a fungal infection. Look out for wetness around the vent which means the parrakeet has diarrhoea and will be dehydrated, and check to see if it is well fleshed each side of the breast bone, which should not feel narrow, sharp and pronounced. A seriously ill bird can loose flesh most rapidly from these large muscles, even in the length of a few hours.

Check also for signs of external parasites, skin and feather disease, which should be obvious. Look for bites or cuts on the face, bill, head, legs and feet; this could indicate bullying on the part of the bird's mate or other individuals being kept in the same flight. Blindness is another unfortunate but possible occurrence; look carefully into the bird's pupils for any tiny white spots or cloudiness within the interior of the eye itself. Care must be taken when feeling the crop to make sure that the bird has been feeding, and also if the contents are in a solid immovable block - which may mean crop binding - or if the crop is bloated with liquid, indicating a crop infection (sour crop). Do not pinch the crop but treat it gently, and see if its surface is red, bruised, wrinkled, and shrunk which indicates disease of the upper digestive system.

Check for an excess of pin feathers and feathers still in their sheaths showing that the parrakeet is in the moult (timely or otherwise) and may have become chilled because of the resulting loss of underdown. Listen for sounds of wheeziness or rasping coming from the nasal area or the lungs, but do not place your ear too close to the bird's bill - I have had mine nipped several times! Examine the lower abdomen of hens - with great care and exerting no pressure - to see if they are swollen with eggs and might be eggbound or, where no obvious swelling is present, feel if the pelvic bones are wide open as proof of breeding condition. Examine both sexes for lumps anywhere that could be tumours; and any bead like whitish lumps that might be the swollen body of an attached feeding tick.

Looking for Causes

So much information can be gleaned in just a few minutes and these valuable clues will help the attendant in pin pointing the cause of the trouble; if a veterinarian is needed, being able to offer a list of symptoms and a detailed description of the condition of the patient will save precious time in coming to a diagnosis.

If definite symptoms exist, it must be worth considering if any of the other parrakeets among the stock exhibit the same characteristics as the one that is sick, which could mean that an infection is spreading and might become an epidemic. It is a good idea to make enquiries whether there are any diseases among pigeon and poultry flocks in the district - whether private or commercial.

Check on the flight and shelter for such things as: flaking on new galvanised mesh or plentiful flakes of rust, new timber which may be impregnated with a strong fungicidal preservative, evidence of mice or other vermin (spreaders of disease), unusual and unknown plants or substances that have grown or been introduced to the birds' living area; anything stagnant or decaying on the roof, examine the contents of the food and water dishes - and the droppings.

It is not as rare as might be thought for segments of tape worm to be found in the faeces of recently imported psittacines. If blood is present in the droppings many things can be suggested: a severe chill, parasitic worms, infectious disease, or an internal haemorrhage perhaps due to a collision with the fabric of the aviary after a scare.

Many novice parrakeet owners place great relevance on the colour of the darker part of their birds' droppings (that which has passed fully through the intestines), believing that the bird is unhealthy if this is anything but black. However, this is not so, the colour of this waste material can vary from light green to dark brown and simply shows what has been consumed - the darker it is the more solid seed has been eaten, the lighter and greener it is the more fruit, vegetable and greenfood has been eaten. The 'white' part of the faeces is waste from the kidneys, passed through ducts which enter into the cloaca (just inside the vent); in diseased birds, this material can be yellowish or buff in colour and can indicate problems such as serious bacterial/viral infection, or even nephritis of the kidneys.

Once a sick bird has been established in the warm room for a few hours, the lack of droppings rather than the presence of copious amounts is of most concern because it could mean that there is a blockage in the gut. Continued droppings of a very high water content also give cause for worry because this means that the patient is becoming increasingly dehydrated.

It is important not to panic and best to first seek obvious, simple reasons for the parrakeet's illness before rushing to open the latest book on all the newest and most dread bird diseases known to veterinary science. The first cause that always comes to mind is that of internal worms, but if the patient has been recently administered a vermifuge, this is one worry at least that can be eliminated. Internal worms are a problem that may be present the year round; the same applies to chills, birds may become chilled winter or summer - but particularly during the moult. When a muggy autumn day is followed by a frosty night, young birds and late moulters - which have a sparse underdown - are at increased risk of chilling.

The winter brings its own problems for birds which need to be kept in outside flights. If the aviaries have enclosed shelters attached, it is best to shut the birds in on nights when there is a thick fog, to avoid cases of pneumonia. If the winter is mild there is more danger of bacteria and viruses being spread by rodents, wild birds, and even on the wind. If the winter is bitter, losses can be caused purely by the combination of low temperatures and nights which are too long; but providing heat and light to healthy Rosellas in an attempt to offset this problem only throws their biological clock askew and makes them come into breeding condition at the wrong time of year or brings about an unseasonable moult.

Especially in winter, if the food supply has not been topped up at least an hour before roosting time, the likelihood of parrakeets succumbing because of empty crops is strong - the smaller the species the higher the risk. Water which becomes frozen during the day must be knocked out of the dishes and replenished so that the birds can continue to drink without resorting to eating ice; birds eat and drink more in severe weather because they need more fuel to provide the energy to keep them warm.

De-worming Psittacine Birds

Newcomers to the keeping and breeding of psittacine birds are not usually aware of the serious dangers presented to their birds by internal parasites. The Roundworm *(Ascaridia columbae)* caused very serious losses in years gone by, and it is true to say that these worms have caused more deaths in Australian parrakeets than in most other parrots; internal worms can even cause the deaths of young birds before they fledge the nest. The parent birds may pick up infected material as they forage on aviary or shelter floor, and pass this on to their young within regurgitated food - after a few weeks the nestlings are heavily infested.

There is no need for losses to be allowed to occur. Administering medication - or even liquid food - via a syringe and catheter tube is a necessary skill for the breeder to master. After a practical demonstration by an experienced aviculturist, and some practice, it is possible to dose psittacines straight into the crop with a reliable de-worming agent. If you are nervous about handling birds yourself and can find no one to do the job, it is possible to add at least one type of de-wormer to the drinking water. However, even though this method is better than no treatment at all, it is a hit and miss affair; the parrakeets may not drink sufficient, or indeed any of the treated water. Even if a completely tasteless chemical is used there is still a strong element of uncertainty.

Roundworms

Roundworms are like earthworms in appearance, but much thinner, and can grow in the host's intestines to a length exceeding two inches (50mm). The worm lays its eggs while in the host, these are passed out in the bird's excrement, continuing the cycle and causing reinfestation. The microscopic eggs are tough and resilient, and can only be destroyed if the entire flight is scorched with a flame gun or blow-lamp - and then only if they lay on exposed surfaces. Those eggs exposed to strong sunlight for long periods will dry up and be destroyed, but those protected in shady, damp positions or just beneath the surface of an earth floor, will survive to perpetuate the adult parasite.

Damp, warm conditions activate the development of the eggs into their necessary pre-host stage. In an attempt to eliminate the eggs, the top four inches (100mm) of earth floors may be carefully removed, or drastic treatment of surfaces with caustic soda might be considered - but obviously, there is danger in using such fierce chemicals as this. Ordinary disinfectants are ineffective, and - in any case - open topped aviaries invite reinfection from wild birds.

Irritation, inflammation and lesions are inflicted on the debilitated parrakeet's intestines as the worms grow and apparently feed off the gut lining and its contents, but the greatest danger comes about when the worms increase to such a number as is sufficient to cause a blockage and rupture of the intestine, in which case the death of their host follows rapidly. The smaller the species of parrakeet, the quicker this is likely to occur.

Treatment

Treatment carried out at regular intervals will prevent unnecessary deaths. For many years we have treated all our birds once in the autumn, once in mid-winter and again a few weeks before each species' usual breeding season. We dose each whole family (parents included) as soon as the youngsters are confident in the flight, though not necessarily independent of their parents. Subsequent clutches are treated in the same manner and all birds sold are dosed directly into the crop a day or two previous to collection by their new owners. This programme is carried out as a preventive measure, regardless of evidence or non-evidence of the presence of worms. If worms can be seen in the birds' droppings after dosing, the affected birds should be treated again after a period of about three weeks.

'Nilverm'/'Nemicide'

Levamisole hydrochloride is the active constituent of *'Nilverm'*; the yellow coloured liquid de-worming agent contains 7.5% w/v *levamisole hydrochloride BP*. It must be protected from heat and light, and stored at a temperature not exceeding 21 deg. C (70 deg. F). It is effective against mature and developing immature stages of all major stomach and bowel worm species, and lung worms. *'Nemicide'* is a clear sterile solution also containing the same active constituent to the same concentration as *'Nilverm'*. However, specifications of veterinary products can be changed, check with your vet to make sure that the strength of the above products have not been altered.

If you have only a small number of parrakeets, it is best to try to purchase enough *'Nilverm'* to last for only six months at a time - the standard pack contains 525ml and is expensive to waste, your local veterinarian may be persuaded to split a pack. *Levamisole* acts so efficiently that some breeders complain of losses due to blockage of the gut, where infestation is extremely heavy - this has never happened to any of our birds during the many years we have used *'Nilverm'*. Worm eggs in the host's gut are said to escape the effects of *levamisole*. *'Nemicide'/'Nilverm'* has an extremely bitter taste.

The following doses, using a solution of **one part of 'Nilverm'** to **four parts of water** have been used on our own birds in past years.

Large to medium species of Rosella	*1ml*
Stanley	*.75ml*

However! And this is most important; in recent years - with a low to nil occurrence of worms - we have found that *only half* of the above dosage has been equally effective for *our* birds in *our* situation; for example, .25ml of a 1:4 solution proved suitable for Lovebirds (which we had previously been giving .50ml), and we reduced the amount given to the rest of our psittacines accordingly - for us this has worked well.

Dosing into the Crop

The solution is administered via a disposable syringe with catheter tube attached; syringes and catheters in various sizes can be obtained from your local veterinarian; a catheter of 2mm external diameter (usually with a yellow nub) is suitable for small psittacines - the size of Lovebirds to Rosellas. As the tip of the catheter is closed with holes in the side, we cut this off and make it smooth either by holding it momentarily in a naked flame or sanding it off with fine emery cloth. This prevents any sharp edges from grazing the insides of mouths or throats. Be warned that the flesh of young birds is very tender and easily damaged by a clumsy action. The catheter should not be cut so short that the bird would be able to swallow it completely if it were pulled from the syringe - this can happen.

The birds are best de-wormed in the morning so that their activities through the day will encourage the speedy movement of any worms through their intestines. If the birds are treated late in the day or in the evening and they have a large accumulation of worms, a blockage may result - at roost their bodily functions are slowed down. Also, any parrakeets that may become sick due to the upset of being caught and handled will not be noticed, and may be lost over night.

The catching of the parrakeets must be done quickly and with the minimum of fuss. In the case of the smaller species of Rosella which can be easily enclosed in the hand, care must be taken not to restrict the abdomen and cause suffocation while concentrating on the tricky job being carried out. It is most important to catch hold of the *parrakeet* before it catches hold of *you!* If it is allowed to bite, the handler is likely to damage it by a reflex action.

I find the best way to hold a small to medium sized parrakeet is with its back in the palm of my left hand, while firmly - but without squeezing - restraining its head from movement by placing thumb and second finger each side of its head - just below the eyes - while my index finger is placed on top of its head. Explaining how to hold a bird may sound condescending, but I have found that birds offered for purchasers to examine in their own hands are most often refused, or held in an awkward manner.

Until complete confidence is gained, it may be necessary to use a gag to hold open the parrakeet's mandibles - a smooth piece of thin stick of suitable dimensions will do. This may be held in position between the second and third fingers of the left hand. After some practical experience, manipulation becomes more dextrous and the bird's reactions fully anticipated, and the use of the gag can be omitted.

The right hand is free to manipulate the catheter into the corner of the bird's mouth, over the tongue and down the throat. If it does not slip down into the crop easily, it must not be forced under any circumstances. A slight, gentle backward and forward action while keeping the bird's neck as straight as possible will usually cause the channel to become free. It is imperative that the catheter goes right down into the crop and not just inside the throat, otherwise the bird can be easily choked. To make quite sure that this is so, the catheter can be felt through the crop wall, but it is important not to mistake the bird's windpipe for the catheter tube, and also to handle the crop very carefully and not pinch it - the crop is easily bruised and damaged. Should the Rosella gasp, choke or begin to splutter at any part of the proceedings, it must be immediately released, allowed to recover and the dosing abandoned until another day.

The de-worming agent is ejected steadily into the crop, not with a sharp spurt. Again, if choking occurs at this time, or there is a discharge from the nostrils, the bird must be released immediately. Once the dosing has been successfully carried out, the parrakeet is set loose into a cage or shut into its shelter. Paper laid under the perches collects any evidence of infestation; any worms are usually passed four to five hours after dosing - but sometimes not until the following day. After dosing, the catheter and syringe may be sterilized by boiling; when they become slightly worn or gnawed they should be discarded. Some breeders use a

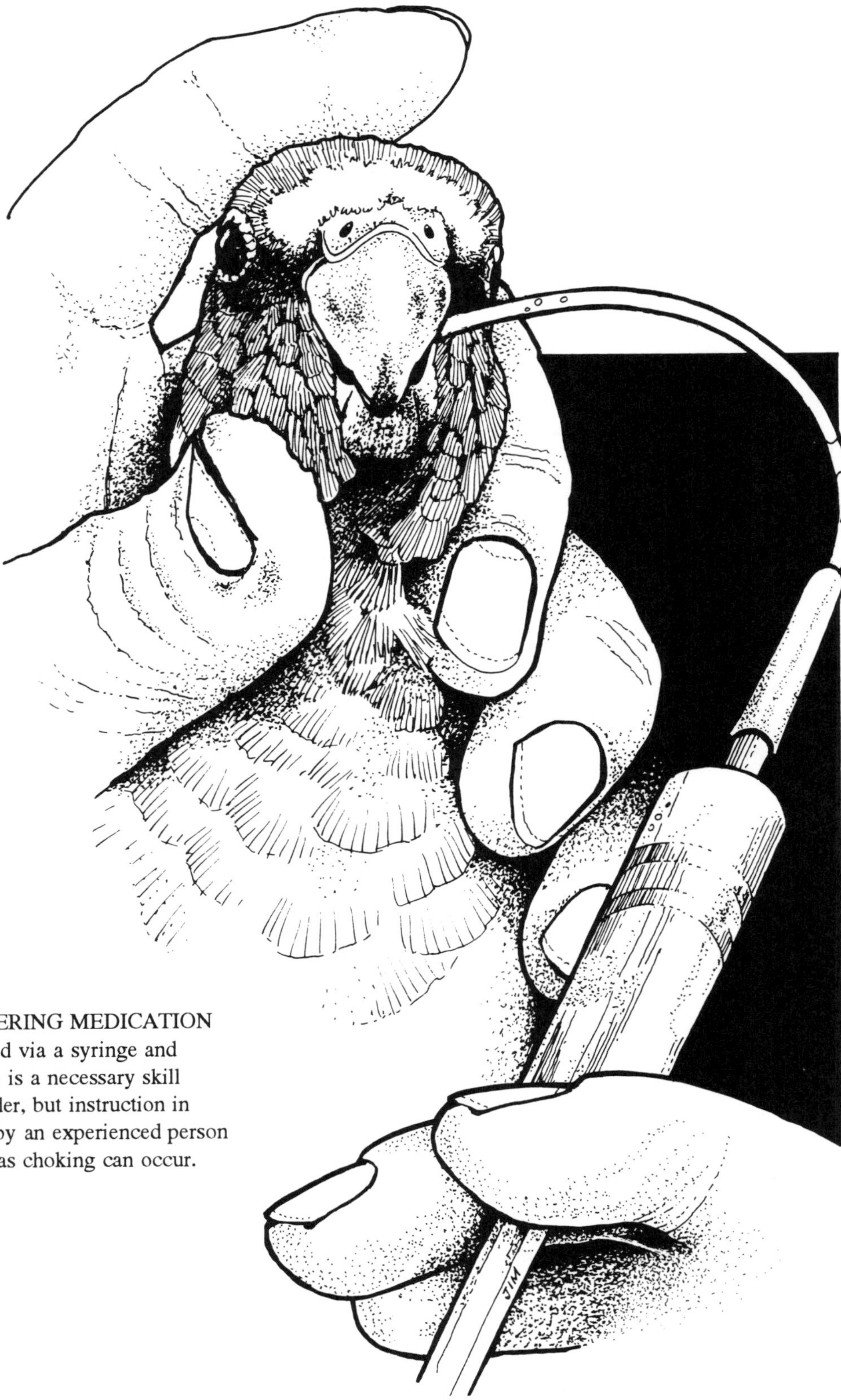

ADMINISTERING MEDICATION or liquid food via a syringe and catheter tube is a necessary skill for the breeder, but instruction in the method by an experienced person is essential, as choking can occur.

Dosing into the Crop via a Syringe & Catheter

rigid crop needle (gavage tube) instead of a catheter; this is a fine hollow metal tube with a blunt nodule or probe at the end.

It should be remembered that undetected infections could be passed through an entire stock if sterilization of the tube is not carried out between the dosing of each bird; alternatively, a new tube and syringe could be used for each parrakeet. If this is not practical and the owner is totally confident that his stock is free of disease, it is still wise to make an attempt at restricting the passing on of infection by cleaning the tube with a mild antiseptic between de-worming each pair or group of birds.

It is dangerous to pour or drip medication directly into a bird's mouth with a spoon, a syringe or a dropper, and can easily lead to death by choking. Also, contrary to usual information, it is possible to inadvertently introduce the catheter into the entrance of a parrakeet's windpipe *(trachea)* and choke it. If the attendant is right handed and holding the bird in the left hand, the catheter is always introduced from the left hand side of the bird's mouth, and slid across to the right hand side of the back of its throat, so as to avoid this danger. The sound of a friendly voice helps sooth the birds while they are being handled.

It is important to make a note of the date when each parrakeet has been dosed and record the results for future reference.

Other De-worming Agents

'Antepar' *(piperazine* - used as a de-wormer for humans) which - though it was used frequently in the past - is not generally recommended nowadays, as it is considered to be ineffective against immature worms and a relatively small amount over the correct dose can be detrimental to the well being of psittacine birds.

'Mebendvet' *(mebendazole)* - a white powder for adding to seed or grain - was very popular at one time because of its simplicity of use. However, some years ago it was found to produce unwelcome side effects on some species of psittacine, and it was recommended that this game bird de-wormer should no longer be used with psittacines.

'Ovorotol' was of European origin; though popular with some parrot keepers, its availability became spasmodic and the active constituent seems to be unrecorded.

'Panacur' *(fenbendazole)* is widely used, it has no taste or smell and can be given in the bird's food or water as well as being administered by dosage. It is claimed that this chemical also kills worm eggs, as well as the worm in all its stages. One note of disquiet came from veterinarian Keith Lawrence in the July 1983 issue of *'Pet Product Marketing'* when he warned that *'Panacur'* was an unsuitable de-wormer for pigeons, as even low dosage rates had caused adverse effects which included feather abnormalities, and that high dosage had caused severe vomiting in these birds. In *'Rosellas'* (published by *Australian Birdkeeper* 1988) Australian veterinarian Dr Rob Marshall warned that this chemical may cause feather problems with Rosellas if given during the moult. He advised that *'Panacur'* (2.5) could be given in the bird's drinking water at a rate of 5ml/litre and should be changed daily for five days. See your own veterinarian to confirm this ratio and also to obtain the correct individual dosage rate when administered into the crop.

'Avermec' *(Ivermectin)* is described by Dr Marshall as so potent that a drop placed on the skin of the back of the neck of a small parrot is sufficient to destroy internal worms. It has to be diluted 100 times with *propylene glycol.* This chemical is also supposed to kill all external parasites, such as mite (including scaly face mite), lice, fleas and ticks, as well as internal worms; taking its potency into account, it would seem wise for the attendant to wear thin rubber gloves when dosing. The comparatively new product known in this country simply as *'Ivermectin'* is now being used by some breeders at a dose of $^1/_4$ml (.25ml) on the skin at the back of the neck; however, it is *most important* that clear concise veterinary advice and instruction on suitability, dosage and instruction should be sought before using this or any other relatively new product.

Hairworms

Hairworms *(Capillaria)* can also invade psittacine birds and are considered to be more debilitating in their effect than roundworms. I have seen it written that chickweed should never be given to psittacines because this widely used green food will cause infestation of hairworm. Having used chickweed as a food for birds over a lifetime of bird keeping and never finding hairworms to have been a problem, I cannot agree with this idea. Nevertheless, wild picked green food should be washed well before feeding in case of worm contamination (and other infection) by wild birds.

Wire Floors as a Worm Preventative

Wire floored cages and aviaries have been used by parrot breeders in recent years with one of the aims being to eliminate the risk of worms, and thereby avoid the need to dose stock. Even so, one breeder told me that after using wire floors for some years his birds still needed de-worming periodically, and anyway, it does not seem fair to deprive Rosellas from foraging at ground level.

Earth Floors

Earth floors with patches of vegetation or shrubs are ideal environments for parasitical worms, and will encourage severe infestation in psittacines. Some breeders prefer concrete floors, but this type of surface also has its drawbacks, two of these being the encouragement of harmful moulds, and the provision of refuge for vermin like rats and mice. I have found that small pebbles laid to a depth of about a foot provide the best aviary floor - this can be hosed over and provides good drainage. The top soil is removed before the pebbles ($^1/_2$" - $^3/_4$" diameter, 12mm - 19mm) are laid. Since using this type of floor in our aviaries, problems with internal worms have been negligible - though we still de-worm as a preventive measure.

New Stock

When purchasing new stock, always enquire whether the birds have been recently de-wormed and, if so, when. If it is necessary to treat them yourself, do so after they have settled in satisfactorily - preferably for a few days at least. It is not wise to rely on microscopic examination of droppings for worm eggs as a sign of their presence. Many years ago we purchased two parrakeets which had been declared clear of worms after microscopic examination of faeces by a veterinarian specializing in psittacines; when dosed forty-eight hours after at our aviaries, a massive infestation of roundworms was discovered, and worms were still being passed after three days.

It is sensible not to overcrowd aviaries, as this increases the likelihood of worm infestation and other infectious disease; ground birds (pheasants, quail, etc) should not be placed in the same aviary as psittacines - they are a frequent source of internal parasites and other disease which can be transferred to parrakeets.

Finally, if in doubt, contact a veterinarian for expert advice and up-to-date news on de-worming agents and methods.

More on Disease

Veterinarians specializing in psittacine birds (or for that matter any cage or aviary birds) used to be few and far between, but from a period roughly dating from the late nineteen seventies when surgical sexing first began to be popular, a number of practitioners realized the potential in this field; nowadays specialist bird vets are not so rare, and at the time of publication of this book, *'Cage & Aviary Birds'* and *'Birdkeeper'* magazines can supply their readers with a long list of specialist bird vets situated up and down the country. So if the bird keeper suspects a serious problem, expert help is much more easier to find and should be quickly sought. In recent years, European regulations have affected greatly the way that British vets have to work, and drugs cannot now be prescribed unless the bird or birds have been examined or aviaries inspected at least once a year; the same European regulations have also meant the loss of some previously widely used veterinary products and drugs.

The main serious health worries with parrakeets used to revolve around the control of parasitical worms, and the two threats of **chlamydiosis** (i.e. parrot disease, psittacosis or ornithosis) and **Newcastle disease** ('fowl pest', which is a notifiable disease because of its danger to the poultry industry, and is subject to a MAFF policy of slaughter of infected and contact birds).

Both diseases are communicable to humans, but the chlamydia organism (some describe it as a parasite, others as a bacterium *or* virus) can be carried by all types of birds - not just parrots which always get the blame - as well as other domestic pets and farm animals (e.g. cats and sheep). In humans the infection is serious, needs immediate medical attention and shows symptoms similar to a severe bout of influenza, but it is just as likely to be caught from ducks or the feral pigeons in towns and cities as it is from psittacines. The disease can be treated with specific antibiotics; it is usually warned that 'cured' birds can remain carriers and spread the infection by shedding the parasitical organisms (which build up at times of stress) through sneezing and in their droppings - I do not know if infected humans also remain carriers after treatment. In parrakeets, symptoms include bloody diarrhoea, discharge from the nostrils, conjunctivitis and disinterest in food. One British parrakeet breeder who had a serious epidemic in his aviaries some years ago told me that infected birds could easily be identified by a vivid yellow content in their droppings; *vibramycin* was used successfully in this outbreak. Around the same period another breeder lost a cock Barnard's Parrakeet whose symptoms included droppings of a 'fluorescent yellow colour', a second cock died showing the same symptoms and was found to have a virus which at the time was rife in continental pig farms - the birds had originated from a continental supplier. *Penicillin* injections into the breast muscle saved another hen bird of the same group which had become ill, and birds in adjacent flights were not affected.

Some years ago there were outbreaks of Newcastle disease in poultry units in the south midlands, and I was advised by my local vet to take the simple precaution of placing by the gate a bowl of *washing soda crystals* diluted in water, for visitors to dip their boots and shoes; I was told this was effective in destroying the Newcastle organism, but was not reassured when warned that the air vents in infected poultry houses sent the disease high in the air, and the wind could spread the infection for many miles by droplet - luckily, no aviaries in the area were affected at the time.

By coincidence, the greater involvement of vets in the health of cage and aviary birds has been accompanied by a crop of 'new' diseases. **Psittacine beak and feather disease (PB&FD)** can affect all psittacines including Rosellas; though it is at its most severe in its symptoms and most commonly seen in Cockatoos, in which the feathers become sparse, brittle, disintegrate and are not replaced as the stubs are moulted; the nails and bill become overgrown and soft. It is caused by a virus, is slow working, highly contagious from bird to bird and from nest material, and - though progress is being made on a vaccine - is at present incurable. Infected material and boxes should be burnt and aviaries thoroughly disinfected.

Polyomavirus first came to notice in the nineteen eighties as a disease of fledgling Budgerigars (i.e. BFD, Budgerigar fledgling disease), and the first known outbreak is believed to have occurred in Britain in nineteen eighty-four. It seems to be mostly a disease of nestlings and young birds, and in nestlings it is noticed by symptoms of diarrhoea, regurgitation of food, shrivelled feet, swollen abdomen and haemorrhage under the skin; body tremor and loss of balance is indicative, and death generally occurs within two days of the onset. With some birds, the polyomavirus can often result in sudden deaths; apparently some birds are more resistant than others and can recover, but indications are that they remain carriers and under times of stress shed the virus, which is extremely infectious and easily picked up by other birds in the vicinity; it is highly resistant to heat, freezing, solvents and only some disinfectants are effective in its destruction. At present no cure is available but researchers believe that a vaccine can ultimately be produced.

Megabacteriosis is now wide spread in British Budgerigar stocks and likely to spread to other parrakeets and parrots; the disease is said to stop the production of acids necessary for digestion, and causes inflammation and ulceration of the proventriculus and the gizzard, which becomes soft. This means that the absorption of nutrients is affected and the bird loses flesh and starves to death. Some victims die suddenly and are found to have bled internally, others show signs of vomiting and diarrhoea. Initially, there is a high mortality rate in a stock of birds, and then a partial immunity seems to build up with occasional losses; birds left alive are believed to remain carriers which develop and spread the disease when subjected to stress. It has been suggested that the bacteria gain a hold *after* the break down of the production of digestive juices, and experimentation of dosing high levels of *hydrochloric acid* seems to have had some beneficial effect - as also the antibiotic *amphotericin B*. This antibiotic has to be given every twelve hours for ten days, but if under dosed the megabacteria quickly becomes resistant.

Cloacal papillomas (genital warts caused by a virus) are another relatively new disease to British aviculture; if the growth of tissue is not noticed in its early stages and cauterized, but left until it has grown so large that it protrudes from the vent, the bird's breeding potential is ruined; at present it seems to be specifically a disease of Macaws - but other bird species have had these eruptions on the skin and legs. **Proventricular dilation syndrome (PDS)**, has appeared in large parrots such as Macaws; birds starve because the condition causes the proventriculus to shrink and food passes undigested - the symptoms of undigested seed in droppings has been seen in Australian parrakeets.

Disease can be caused by many organisms: bacteria (e.g. **salmonellosis, avian tuberculosis**), viruses (e.g. **paramyxovirus** affects the brain and causes wryneck - twisting of the neck - a vaccine has been developed in Holland), fungi/yeast/mould (e.g. **candidiasis** and **aspergillosis**), protozoa (e.g. **trichomoniasis**, infects the lining of the crop and causes it to shrivel), external parasites (e.g. **various mite, lice** - treatable with *sprays and powders* or *'Ivermectin'*), parasites of the internal digestive organs (e.g. **ascariasis**, treatment previously described; earwigs can carry **tapeworms** and pass them on to birds), and **parasites of the blood**. In Britain, even **midges** which breed in pools of still water (often where there are cattle) have been known to cause the deaths of parrots and parrakeets by biting and infecting them with a blood parasite (a **leucytozoon** - protozoan); the parasite invades white blood cells and causes cysts in muscles such as the gizzard and heart. A similar blood parasite endemic to the tropics has often been found present in imported parrakeets (**akibiasis**).

Pasteurella is an insidious disease spread by rodents and wild birds - in particular mice, greenfinches and sparrows. It is prevalent in cold and damp weather, and can only be diagnosed by postmortem examination and laboratory tests. Of the various symptoms indicative of the disease, the most common is the discolouration (pallid) of the liver, spleen and other internal organs, and presence of lesions, yellowish white spots and abscesses in these organs. The gut is often full of dark blood. The victim dies very quickly with few external symptoms, the droppings are normal, the bird shows a slight malaise, glazing of the eyes and lack of appetite. It dies in a convulsion as it is poisoned by the toxins produced by the disease. If pasteurella is suspected, veterinary advice should be sought immediately as it may be possible to prevent the disease spreading to other stock, or to save other birds incubating the disease by treatment with a specific antibiotic.

'Itraconazole' is a relatively new drug for treating **candidiasis** *(Candida albicans)*, a yeast infection for which *'Nystatin'* and *'Daktarin'* has been recommended in the past. The disease in not greatly prevalent in Rosellas - it is more frequent in Lories and Eclectus Parrots - but should be noted. It often results after a serious illness, attacks the mouth and crop, causing lesions, and can spread to the air sacs; a **deficiency in vitamin A** (which also causes eye problems) or a prolonged course of antibiotics (which causes depletion of vitamins and natural gut flora) usually allows the disease access via infected food, and a course of a good vitamin supplement is an important factor in its treatment. **Moulds** are a definite health hazard, they thrive on damp concrete, are responsible for lung disorders such as **aspergillosis** and - if present in sufficient amount - the toxins they produce can also kill. Itraconazole has also been used with some effect on aspergillosis which causes severe wheezing; the lungs, air sacs and also the liver become invaded by this disease; in the liver it produces toxins which cause rapid poisoning of the victim. Both diseases can be caused through dirty feed dishes and stale food, and spores can be present and thrive in soaked and germinated seed. The brown mould found in rye grass seeds is said to be highly poisonous *(ergot)* and on rare occasions even humans have been known to die when eating rye bread infected with its toxin.

Chills can easily turn to **pneumonia** which causes the bird to gasp and throw its head back as it does so, once this state has been reached it is unlikely to survive, but *ampicillin* has worked on many occasions. This used to be available as *'Penbritin'*, ready to use in a handy syringe type oral doser, but is now unavailable; I have since used *'Clamoxyl'* powder (active constituent *amoxycillin trihydrate* - Beecham) which can be mixed with a couple of drops of water and administered onto the bird's tongue with a dropper. It is impossible to differentiate from the bird's appearance between chilling, with the scouring it causes, and **infectious enteritis**, but the latter needs veterinary advice and treatment with a suitable antibiotic. As previously mentioned, European directives to vets mean that they must see the bird before they can supply drugs, technically, it must be 'in their care'; it is better to get the vet to visit than take the bird to the surgery - immediate attention is advised. It is unwise to give green food to birds with chills and enteritis as it increases the scouring. If the bird is reluctant to feed it may be necessary to hand feed it with the aid of a syringe and catheter tube down the throat and straight into the crop; I have administered antibiotic along with the food if needed, the same food as I have used for hand feeding nestlings, mixed to a creamy consistency so that it could be drawn into a syringe. One or two millilitres only of food was given at each feed, placed about three hours apart, until the bird could feed itself.

Eye infections are not common with Rosellas, but an occurrence should be treated without delay as it may be highly contagious, usually only one eye is affected but it can spread to the other. The advice of a vet should be sought, as eye disease can also be a symptom of chlamydia (psittacosis). Over the years, I have found that *'Neobiotic'* eye ointment *(neomycin sulphate*, Upjohn Ltd), in conjunction with *'Aureomycin' (chlortetracycline hydrochloride)* antibiotic powder given in the drinking water, is the best treatment for eye disease in parrakeets. It is important to put the ointment in *both* eyes, even if only one is affected. Catch the bird, pull down the eye lid (best eye first), run some ointment into the well of the lid, allow to melt, and then close the eye and roll the lid around to spread the ointment over the entire eye ball; do this the other side, and - if severely affected - treat three times a day. As the eye improves, apply the ointment morning and late afternoon. Continue to do this for a few days even after the eye appears normal, as eye problems have a habit of returning if not thoroughly cleared up, the infection may develop an immunity to the antibiotics and then be impossible to clear. With eye disease I have cured in the past, I found it is most important to give the antibiotic - *'Aureomycin' (Cyanamid)* for my choice - in the water all the time the bird was being treated with the ointment. A course of vitamin/mineral supplement on the food was needed during and after treatment. It is best to clear out and disinfect the aviary, and destroy the old perches, to prevent re-infection. Infected birds should be kept in isolation until they are totally cured.

Self **feather biting** is most common in Pennant's and Mealies. Anti-peck sprays may be tried together with provision of extra branches and twigs - to keep their bills occupied - and a roomy flight, but once the habit is acquired there is small chance that it will cease. Feather biting may be initiated by the irritation of external parasites like mite; mite of various species are a pest and health hazard, not only in the irritation and blood sucking they cause but by introduction of infections and blood parasites. They can be kept down by using the various mite sprays that are available, by painting the woodwork with paraffin, and burning out nest-boxes periodically with a blowlamp. *'Alugan'* - a powder which was diluted in water - was a very useful acaricide when used as a wash over woodwork and wire, but seems to have become unobtainable - possibly through the new European regulations.

Where a *serious* disease is suspected, dead birds should be sent for **post-mortem**; the advice generally given by veterinary practioners is that the fresh carcass must be wetted down (to eliminate the insulatory properties of the plumage), wrapped in paper, sealed in a plastic bag, kept cool in a refrigerator and got to the veterinary surgery or laboratory within three days - if longer, then placed in the freezer. Whether it would be wise to put a bird which had possibly died from an unknown disease in the same refrigerator/freezer as the food for the family is questionable to say the least!

Reassurance

Enough of the morbid subject of dread disease, but some final words which I hope will give reassurance. We rarely use disinfectant around the aviaries, because of the unknown dangers of birds ingesting spillage of such chemicals, and because their superfluous use could cause harmful organisms to develop immunity; we keep things as clean as possible without risking disturbing breeding pairs, and yet, since changing from a mixture of importing/exporting/dealing/breeding over twenty years ago to solely *breeding* and selling our own surplus birds at home and abroad, we have had no serious disease problems - so why try to put something right when there is nothing wrong? The loss of a bird is a very rare occurrence, and birds seldom become ill; the only medications we *always* keep handy are *'Clamoxyl'* in case of lung disorders when there is freezing fog, *'Neobiotic'* ointment for damaged eyes, *'Aureomycin'* for dusting wounds and as a wide spectrum antibiotic, and *'Nilverm'* to keep our birds clear of parasitical worms; *'Nilverm'* is the product used most and then only about three to four times a year, as a preventive. We make sure we have no infestations of mice, that the food is fresh and of good quality, and that the water is kept clean and fresh; we have obtained no outside stock for our main specialized strains of psittacines in over twenty years, but we have parrakeets still breeding that have been here in excess of twenty five years, and still look as healthy and young as the grand-children and great-grand-children they have preceded.

Probiotics, symbiotics, electrolyte solutions, filtered water, pelleted foods, special disinfectants that can kill all microbes known to humanity at fifty paces, they may be marvellous products for all I know, but how *did* we manage to do without them, yet still breed enough good birds to make a living and maintain the breeding stock all this time? My advice is: to make use of new products and methods when they are well proven; when you have a good stock of birds be very cautious about adding more; do not over stock, overcrowding increases the risk of disease; keep parasites and vermin under control and keep everything as clean and tidy as posssible without being obsessive and upsetting nesting birds. Certainly be wary of the risk of introducing disease - but do not allow yourself to become paranoid.

Index

Index of Species & Sub-species Scientific Names:
(Colour Illustrations in **bold**).

Index of Species & Sub-species English Names:
(Colour Illustrations in **bold**).

General Index:
(Page numbers of Colour Illustrations in **bold**, and Line Illustrations and Photographs in *Italics*).

Magazines and Societies which often include information on Rosellas and associated parrakeets:

Cage & Aviary Birds Magazine, King's Reach Tower, Stamford Street, London SE1 9LS, England.

Birdkeeper Magazine, King's Reach Tower, Stamford Street, London SE1 9LS, England.

The Parrot Society, 108b Fenlake Road, Bedford MK42 0EU, England.

Australian Birdkeeper, PO Box 6288, Tweed Heads South, NSW 2486, Australia.

Avicultural Society of Australia, 52 Harris Road, Elliminyt, Victoria 3249, Australia.

Avizandum, David & Vera Dennison, PO Box 1758, Link Hills, Natal 3652, South Africa.

Dansk Fuglehold, Mogens Stig Andersen, Faergevej 17, Postboks 101, 3600 Frederikssund, Denmark.

Parkieten Societeit, A. Piersma, Joh. Frisostraat 13, 9285 TS Buitenpost, Holland.

Books recommended for further reference:

The Manual of Colour Breeding, Jim Hayward (J.& P. Hayward).

Australian Parrots, Forshaw & Cooper (Lansdowne).

Australian Parrakeets, Dr H.D. Groen (Groen).

Australian Parrakeets and their Colour Mutations, Herman Kremer (Kremer).

A Guide to Rosellas, (Australian Birdkeeper).

A Guide to Australian Long & Broad-tailed Parrots, Kevin Wilson (Australian Birdkeeper).

Parrots of the World, Forshaw & Cooper (Lansdowne).

Parrots their Care & Breeding, Rosemary Low (Blandford).

Lexicon of Parrots, Thomas Arndt (Arndt)

Information on exporting members of Platycercus, Barnardius and Purpureicephalus (Appendix II species which need export licences and health certificates):

Department of the Environment (Wildlife Licensing), Tollgate House, Houlton Street, Bristol. BS2 9DJ

Ministry of Agriculture, Fisheries & Food (Animal Health), Government Buildings, Hook Rise South, Tolworth, Surbiton, Surrey. KT6 7NF